EULOGY OF CHILDHOOD MEMORIES

By Mark Crandall

Design and Format by Gen Y Creative
www.genycreative.com

Editorial support provided by Kat Hinson, Gen Y Creative, Andrea T. Stanford, Jason A. Archambeault, Megan Crandall

ISBN 978-0-692-97841-2

FOREWORD

On some cold Friday night, sometime close to a decade ago, I was standing outside the New Hampshire Art Institute in Manchester, New Hampshire feeling the kind of cool wetness that arrives in the air on New England evenings when autumn is catching up to the last days of summer. I was at an event called "Inspired Recovery." Inspired Recovery was an early, burgeoning attempt to celebrate the addiction recovery community in Manchester. The evening featured art, music, and spoken word poetry produced by persons in recovery to tell the story of recovery through the arts. For several years, this was the only event in New Hampshire that promoted what is known as National Recovery Month. The event did a reasonable job gathering visual art and music. Unfortunately, we weren't able to attract spoken word poets that really connected with our recovery community, until that night.

That was the night I met Mark Crandall. I remember listening to Mark's poetry along with a few hundred other people who were riveted by his powerful, truthful, raw message; when he was done performing, I felt like I'd been in a fight. His poetry moved me to look at his pain and reflect on my own. To hear about his history and remember the past from which my life emerged. I could see how he connected with young people, how they wanted to hear him share from a place of deep introspection and, of course, hope. I left the performance hall and walked outside. Almost unconsciously, as if emerging from a room set afire into that cool refreshing air touched by the smell of changing leaves, I found myself outside reconnecting with the events of the evening. As I listened to people reflecting on the performance they'd just witnessed, I could see people being touched by poetry in a way I'd never seen before. After a moment of catching my breath, I turned to go back into the event and that's the moment I met Mark Crandall.

In the years since, I've been fortunate see some of the amazing things Mark has accomplished. Every time I talk to Mark, there are remnants of that first night. As then, now he continues to speak truth, to explore, expose, and explain the roots of his life and the way this life is connected to the person he is today. Each time we connect, I find myself reflecting on the conversation and carrying parts of our dialogue into the other relationships that mean the most to me in this life. Now the readers of this book will have the opportunity to touch the same experience I did all those years ago as it has evolved into the book you are about to read. I promise you, the story you are about to hear will change and challenge you to think about where you've been and how, no matter the circumstance, our better angels can prevail.

Marty Boldin

CHAPTER ONE -

WHY'D YOU LEAVE ME?

Fixated by fairy tales
Separating them all
Built with strong nails
Only to watch the structure fall

My earliest memories—some of the darkest and most difficult of my childhood—are not those I would wish on any child, especially one so young.

I remember a night from when I was two-and-a-half years old, I was placed in the living room of some unknown house to watch television, I remember that I was not interested in the entertainment on the screen at all. This was a common scenario for me. I have several memories of being in unfamiliar locations with a feeling of being alone. As strange as it may seem, I remember finding comfort in the feelings that were produced from being alone. This is a strong thread that continues throughout the entirety of my life.

I heard a commotion in the back room. I remember not wanting to look back, as I felt I would get into trouble if I saw what was taking place. For several moments, I fought the urge to become aware. When I couldn't resist any longer, I looked. At the time, I was unsure of what I saw. Several years later, I knew that what I had witnessed was my mother and some unknown folks snorting a powdery substance off a chest freezer. Once I saw my mother and was assured that she hadn't left me again, I went back to watching the show. Even as a child, I was never satisfied with what was present in my life; I was always searching for just a little something else. Something to take the pain away, to dull the thoughts, to place me somewhere other than the here and now.

At about the same time, I remember waking up in an apartment in Claremont, New Hampshire, which happens to

as born on November 3, 1983. I remember seeing
ing on the floor playing with her dollhouse. There
n my stomach, a strong yearning that something
.rong. Well, something was wrong! That something
was that I could not recall the last time I had eaten. I was so
hungry (take this as a fact or a metaphor). I asked my sister
where mommy was. She said, "They are at the diner across
the street eating." I punched her dollhouse and started crying
hysterically.

- Mommy left again.
- Mommy wasn't coming back.
- This world was already so unfair for someone so young.

This moment began building the foundation for how I
would live my life for many years to come. Where was mine?
When was I going to get fed? There was a yearning that drove
me to insanity.

Shortly after this, my sister had been placed in a
bathtub for a bath and nearly drowned as a result of my
mother leaving her in there. My grandmother found her and
called 9-1-1. Learning of that moment many years later, it
seemed like a great basis for hatred, and it became just that.
The Department of Children, Youth and Families (DCYF) was
contacted, and my sister was taken from my mother, as they
had enough evidence for a finding of child neglect.

Shortly after my sister was taken away, I have a memory
of sitting at a another unknown kitchen table eating some
delicious fruity cereal. A strange woman notified my mother
of a phone call she had just received. My mother's reaction
was one of anger and fear. She ran out of the house screaming
and crying. This must have been a common occurrence, as I
remember not even slowing down the process of shoveling
cereal into my mouth. Actually, the cereal seemed to taste
better.

I believe the phone call that instilled panic in my
mother was from DCYF—they were looking to take me from

her as well. Of course, at the time I hadn't the slightest idea what this meant, nor could I anticipate the amazing blessings that would unfold as a result. A few weeks later, I was placed in the same foster home that my sister had been placed in.

Many years later I confirmed that the call my mother received was DCYF notifying her that she needed to bring me in to them because they had a home for me. The strange house that I was in at the time was somewhere in New York. My mother had fled New Hampshire in an attempt to keep me in her custody. DCYF had called the foster parents who took my sister and asked if they would consider taking me as well. They agreed. My foster mother said that I showed up to her house wearing pajamas I had outgrown and carrying a small trash bag full of belongings, none of which fit or were useful to a child who was going to stay away from home.

For several years, I heard nothing of my mother. I spent so much time trying to answer the riddle of why. Why hadn't I heard from her? Is this love? Imagine pondering thoughts like these at the age of four. I later learned that she sent us cards and drew us pictures. My foster parents were concerned about the impact it would have on my sister and me, so they withheld them. I know now that they did this because of the inconsistency of my mother's contact and the empty promises that she spilled on each page she sent. It did appear that our mother seemed to have more interest in us while we were gone than she ever did when we were in her custody.

Reflecting back, I did not know or understand what was going on during this time. The only thing that kept playing in my head was that mommy had left again. It has taken years of spiritual practices, therapy and a number of various transformation courses for me to now have some freedom and some compassion for what she was going through. I took it all out on her. Where the fuck was my father? Why didn't he take any of the hatred shots I so often fired at her?

At this point, I unknowingly made a vow to never be hurt by another woman, and in an attempt to protect myself from feeling abandoned again, would sabotage every subsequent relationship, no matter the magnitude of the repercussions. Although I was placed in the care of a loving and embracing family, I couldn't feel the love that they shared. I just knew deep down that they would leave me at some point. Everyone had up until this point, so how could this be any different? I remember staying with my new grandparents while my foster parents worked on leveling land for the new trailer that they purchased. Unaware of it at the time, I was to be raised in this trailer—outside of trips to institutions and other fine establishments intended to rehabilitate unwanted children such as myself.

I also had no idea at the time that these memories, although scattered and vague, were the beginning of an umbrella of self-pity and hatred I would live under for more than 20 years. In the following chapters, I will discuss various situations I found myself in as a result of playing the victim—blaming every action that I took on events from my past—while fighting an unwavering internal battle. If only I had the outlook then that I have now, I could have saved so many loving people from the heartache and turmoil that was left in the wake of my destruction, set in motion by my determination to take what I felt the world owed me. The downside, or upside, depending on your perspective, is that if I had made different choices, I might not have walked as far through hell as I did and surely would not be as strong as the man writing this today.

—— CHAPTER TWO ——

SOMETHING IS WRONG WITH THIS ONE

Lay me down and tuck me in
Played the game and couldn't win
An expensive lesson I had to learn
Every bridge crossed I chose to burn

Imoved to Enfield, New Hampshire, when I was three years old. This wasn't my choice, but surely the safest option. Actually, I had no say at all. As previously stated, DCYF took me from my mother's care and placed me in a foster home. When I say, "took me," I mean saved me from greater suffering at the hands of my drug-addicted mother. Cocaine, men, and no father are the lasting memories of my early childhood. Today I have come to understand that they did the best they could with what they had; and what they had was a hand similar to the one I was dealt.

Except for hunger (a constant yearning to fill the aching internal void within), I'm unclear of any fluent thoughts until around the age of seven years old. This is when I started to become convinced that I was different from everyone else. *Kids do not want to be different.*

Most people can only imagine what it is like for a seven-year-old to try to explain to his classmates that he doesn't know his real parents, especially when he doesn't fully understand it himself. I tried to comprehend the role that these "fill-in parents" were playing. I used to tell the other kids in class that my mommy was going to come back and get me soon. These bad people took me away from her. Because of all the medications I was already taking, even at this age, I would pretend that I was some kind of science experiment, and the findings of the research being conducted were held on another planet.

"Try this counselor with this combination of

medications. He surely has ADD and Bi-Polar Disorder. Something is wrong with this one."

Not knowing what any of this meant, I just wanted my mom and dad to come back and get me.

Living with my foster parents was strange. I always had food to eat, which although I couldn't put it together at the time, was new. I used to eat entire boxes of honey buns, and other fat kid snacks. It was as if in my mind I needed to eat as much as possible because I was unsure of whether or not the food would run out. My new parents never said anything; they just kept buying more and more snacks. However, no matter how much I ate, I never got full.

I began to develop a low self-image. It was difficult for me to pull my shirt off around other kids. I wasn't fat, but I had developed a little gut. This is more than likely due to all the oatmeal cream pies and honey buns I had consumed over the past three years. I struggled to fit in. I was enrolled in soccer, which I really enjoyed. It wasn't the actual sport that excited me but the hopes of getting to kick another kid in the shin as hard as I could. Watching others suffer brought me a sense of joy, knowing that they would experience even a small piece of what I endured on a daily basis.

Around this time, in kindergarten, I met my first friend. James was a super cool kid, which I couldn't understand. He lived in a trailer just like I did. Many kids poked fun at me for living in a trailer, but not him. After one of our meaningless soccer games he invited me over to his house to play. I remember running around outside with him playing war, which looked like us smacking each other with sticks and using cuss words that I couldn't get away with saying at my own house.

I felt connected to James. All my fears and worries about how the world was going to fuck me over each day went away. Unfortunately, I could not be such a comfort to James. He made the mistake of showing me his Ninja Turtle collection—the most lavish Ninja Turtle collection I had ever seen! He had them all, even the limited-edition ones that I was begging my foster parents to buy me. Nothing they ever bought for me was good enough. No matter how hard they tried, they could never show me enough of the love and affection I craved.

James had one Turtle that I wanted so badly! I tried to convince him to let me borrow it, but I think he knew how shady I was even at such a young age. He would have never seen that Turtle again.

One day when I was picked up from James' house, I remember begging to go to the store to purchase that Turtle. I was told no and that if I wanted to own that Turtle, I needed to save my money to buy it. I never enjoyed being told no (even to this day, it's one of my least favorite answers). On Monday, I went to school as usual. I remember bringing one of my Turtles for show-and-tell. James brought his as well. The little shithead just "happened" to bring the Turtle I wanted to borrow for show and tell. I looked so stupid! James made a fool of me, and that I couldn't let stand.

At recess when all my classmates ran to the door to go play on the playground I headed for the bathroom. My teacher pleaded with me to go outside with the rest of the kids. I said I just need to go potty, and then I'll go outside. She stated that I needed to hurry up and get outside. I agreed with her and went to the bathroom.

I didn't need to go to the bathroom; James needed to suffer. My mission was to take his prized turtle from him, and so I did. I felt excitement. Adrenaline shot through my body as I walked to my coat on the rack to hide the Turtle. When recess was over and everyone came back in the classroom, I tried to "act normal." I was attempting to disguise my devious actions. A few moments passed, and everyone become fixated on the fact that James was crying. He found out that his favorite turtle had vanished. This was my friend. He was one of the only kids who had invited me into their home.

I'm sure most children would have felt a strong sense of guilt or shame, or at the very least, a recognition that stealing is wrong. Me, I felt complete. Any concern about my friend was quickly replaced by an inner joy.

As an adult, I now understand that a child deals with the belief that "everyone will leave me" by preempting that move. By purposely causing someone to leave, you're not the victim. This episode was one of the first in a pattern of pushing people out of my life in an attempt to protect myself from the impending turmoil that I would suffer when they inevitably left.

As my childhood progressed it continually brought me a real sense of satisfaction to watch others suffer. As an adult, I know that often people steal because they need to; I stole because I enjoyed watching people suffer. Watching them go through all the stages of loss.

"Where did it go?"

"I must have lost it."

"It was just here."

"Did you take it?"

"Who me?"

"No way I would never do such a thing."

"Let me help you look for it."

This one experience led to a life of stealing. Sometimes it was an object such as money or clothing. Later, it turned to drugs. My most common theft was emotional security, which was usually stolen from those who cared about me the most.

The first memorable feeling of inadequacy struck me hard in the first grade. I remember sitting at the little tables joking with some kids in class. We always read out loud from a book right before naptime. I really enjoyed naptime. Jocelyn and I would lie beside each other and pretend we shared the love of two movie stars. Well, at least that's what I pretended; who knows what was going on in her little mind. Somehow, I always seemed to avoid the book making it to me. This day was different. My class clowning was interrupted by the teacher handing me a Dr. Seuss book, and I was asked if I would start the reading.

I started to try to read the words on the page, but couldn't. I stared at the letters on the pages, but couldn't make them into words. Classmates started to laugh as I struggled through the pronunciation of each letter that made up each word. I couldn't do it. I was unable to read. The laughter tore through me like a freight train. The shame and horror I felt was instantly replaced by rage and hatred. I took the book from the table and threw it across the room and launched a chair at the chalkboard. My classmates and teacher were mortified. This situation set the tone for how I would respond to life for many years. When confronted with any challenge, my auto reply was to insert rage. This was demonstrated through a number of uncivil behaviors, which I slowly found out society frowned on.

I was sent to the principal's office for this outburst. Mr. Pebble was a feared man. Very soft spoken with bright red hair. I wasn't even nervous. I actually felt as if I was cared for, as if I was noticed. The reason why I was in his office didn't matter to me. The end result of the conversation was that I now had to attend sessions with a reading tutor. This tutoring was so conveniently taking place during the time of reading in class; this meant that I did not need to worry about the book being passed to me again.

Later that day, all the kids were out on the playground. We were all running around, and one of the kids, Spence, made a comment about how I was unable to read the book in class. I don't remember his exact words, but I do remember the rage that shot through me as the other kids laughed. I picked up a large stick and threw it as hard as I could at Spence. Due to the fact that I wasn't an athlete of any kind, the stick fell short of Spence and struck an innocent a girl who had nothing to do with the situation. It split her head wide open. She started screaming; again, everyone appeared mortified at my outburst. I remember countless people asking what was wrong with me.

Now I was back in Mr. Pebble's office and was notified that my foster father was on his way to pick me up. I was being suspended from school for a week, not the norm for your average eight-year-old. Well, I was clearly not your average child. The suspension actually brought me some comfort. My foster father showed up, and all he said to me was, "get to the car." His punishment for me was to sit in the recliner for the next five hours until my foster mother got home. I don't remember how the situation ended up playing out, but this started the torture that I was to put my foster parents through for the next 17 years.

For the next couple of months, I had to go down into the basement of my school to take a reading practice class. I hated this time each day. The woman that I had to meet with had the smelliest breath ever, and she would sit so close to me that I wanted to vomit. Although extremely uncomfortable, I became motivated to learn how to read, if only to not have to meet with Dragon Breath any longer. That's not her given name, just an assigned pet name. Focusing on people's faults and shortcomings is a tool I embraced early on. I formulated negative opinions about everyone that I came into contact with. These formulations would comfort me as I moved through life. The comfort being that if they were to leave me I had already built up a story to justify the abandonment. Dragon Breath ended up making a recommendation that I be transferred to Canaan Elementary due to their special needs programming. My foster parents complied and agreed with this request, and I became a "SPED." This is what all the kids were called that needed either academic or behavioral assistance in school. Just one more reason to feel inadequate.

—CHAPTER THREE—

NEW, MORE RESPONSIBLE HUMANS

You picked me out of a line
Not knowing what was in store
You chose me and accepted me
Like an eagle one day I would soar

October 31, 1990, was a day that I will remember as long as I live. Outside of the fact that it is my biological mother's birthday and three days before my own, it was the day that my foster parents decided to claim my sister and me. We were adopted.

Of course, at seven years old I had no idea what this meant. I just knew there was a celebration, and everyone kept congratulating me. I was so confused. I was being congratulated because my biological parents could not take care of me, and now some new, more responsible humans were picking up where they left off? This baffled me! Imagine being seven years old and attempting to explain to your classmates what had just transpired, especially when it made no sense to you. I'm unclear on what I said, but I know that my own confusion must have only muddled it for others.

Although the adoption process was one of the most confusing things I went through as a child, it later proved to be the most amazing blessing I could have imagined. Two incredible humans agreed to accept my sister and me into their home and completely uproot their lives to raise us. Sounds easy enough, but knowing what I put each of them through, it is a blessing that I have the relationships that I do with each of them today. My new mother taught me about unconditional love and the power of prayer and positive thinking. My new father taught me how to work hard and provide for your family.

Shortly after the adoption, I was transferred to Canaan

Elementary School to take part in the Special Education Program. I found myself feeling like even more of an outcast now. As a result of the compounding confusion, my behavior spiraled even further out of control. I was on a quest to drive everyone as far away from me as possible and was about to face a whole new group of people to whom I would have to explain what was going on with me and my life, when I couldn't even put it together for myself.

As part of being enrolled in the Special Education Program — or SPED program as the "normal" kids called it — I was able to access the SPED room at any time throughout the day. This was convenient because my behavior was escalating. I would skip classes and roam the halls. I created a number of disturbances, including but not limited to disrupting other classes by being a clown, throwing things, damaging property, assaulting other kids, stealing, and on and on. I learned that if I dropped the SPED card, it would prevent me from receiving consequences for my behavior. I used this to my advantage every opportunity that I had. Whether it was getting out of homework assignments, going out for an extra recess when all the other kids were in class, or avoiding suspensions. It did not take me long to realize that this setback was an extremely beneficial tool.

As I began the new school, I thought I was starting to be accepted by the other children. Instead, it turned out that they were terrified of my extremely unpredictable violent tendencies. I didn't think twice of kicking a kid on the playground, throwing a chair, slide tackling someone in the hallway (a skill learned from my mother's attempt at getting me to play soccer). My group of friends shifted completely. I started to build "meaningful" relationships with all of the other "SPEDs." Most all of whom were engaged in the same "fuck the world" attitude that was taking root in me.

—— CHAPTER FOUR ——

ANYTHING THAT TAKES ME OUTSIDE OF MYSELF

It's not your fault I swear
You weren't taught to care
Opened scars laid bare
Much too painful to share

Around this time, I began to explore my sexuality. Although sexual exploration by children and young adolescents is rarely talked about, I felt that my memoir would lack the integrity of my life if I didn't share some of my experiences. Many of these harmed others and may cause some of my readers to feel a certain way about me. I am okay with this today because I know that these were actions of a confused and curious adolescent and do not represent the man I've become.

My adoptive parents brought several other children into their home during my childhood. I can think of at least 10 who came to live with us. My room was the one that was always shared with these guests. The "roommate" that most sticks out in my mind was my cousin Michael. He was eight or nine years older than I was. At the time, I was around nine, and Michael was 17 or 18 years old. His companionship was the start of my sexual exploration. He demonstrated many things that a nine-year-old probably shouldn't see. We shared bunk beds; of course, I was on the top, since his age trumped mine. I remember countless nights when I would wake up to my bed rocking and sounds of some heinous animal attack down below. I had no clue what this was until my curiosity became overwhelming, and I began to go through Michael's belongings in our shared room.

In his belongings scattered around the room, I found a pile of magazines with nearly naked women on the covers. I remember starting to flip through the pages and something started to happen in my pants. I don't need to go into detail, as I am positive that we all know what goes into the creation of an erection. I had no clue what was going on with my pants situation until I started to explore and quickly realized that if you rubbed it hard and long enough it would go off. The explosion was the most profound experience of my life up to that point. Since my parents worked long days and opposite shifts, I lacked supervision. As with many boys that age, I started to rub my little Willy on anything and everything.

This led to further surveillance of my cousin and his lower bunk sex-capades, the discovery of more and more pornographic material, and telltale stains on nearly everything I owned and some of what others owned. Needless to say, I was far advanced in my knowledge of sex compared to my peers. In school, I always had a girlfriend and would try to re-enact the things that Michael did to his girlfriends. When you are 10 and 11 years old, this is severely frowned on when you are caught. For more background on this, feel free to ask my mother. Poor woman. At age 12, I was dry humping everything in sight. I got caught dry humping a couple of relatives "playing house" and even a six-year-old girl I was forced to babysit a few times.

Of course, I know today that this behavior is not okay and am remorseful for many of my actions as an adolescent. I don't remember ever being educated on what was acceptable sexually and what was not. I remember my adoptive father telling me "wear a condom or you may get something that won't wash off in the shower". I had no idea what that meant at the time, nor did I care. I knew that when I climaxed it made me feel good. As with most of my behavior in my early years, I never stopped to consider the ramifications of my actions on others, I was solely concerned with finding relief.

To this day I am still remorseful for many of my attempts at seeking relief, but do know the importance of educating my children on what is acceptable and what is not. For example, it is not appropriate to go down a girl's pants in first grade. I learned that the hard way with a suspension from school.

Having counseled and coached hundreds of men throughout the years, I now know how common such behaviors are, and also how detrimental they can be to the transformation process of forgiveness. This is the sole reason why I have placed this section in my story.

— CHAPTER FIVE —

SANTA'S NOT COMING

Forever seems so far away
When I can't even end today
Hearing voices, seeing no faces
Demons inside my hunger chases
Open your eyes there's no time to dream
Not everything is the way it may seem

I remember the Christmas Eve of the year my sister and I were adopted—more than any other. We were told that our biological mother was coming to visit us. We hadn't seen or heard from her in years. I remember the excitement. My sister and I were running around the trailer in which we lived, jumping up and down with sheer joy! Every time there were headlights on the road by our house I would run to the sliding glass door to look outside. Each time there was a growing feeling of disappointment, as it was only a car driving by. I can remember my adopted parents making several attempts to draw our attention away from our growing disappointment. They had figured out what we hadn't yet—Mom wasn't coming.

Looking back, my adoptive parents may have been hurt by our excitement, but they also anticipated our inevitable disappointment and hated that we had to experience it. Our biological mother did not come that year. She continued to lay the groundwork for me to be convinced that no one could be trusted. Especially women. They lied. Looking back on it now, and knowing all about the addiction, I know she probably wanted to show up. If she were suffering from addiction, as I would later, no matter how badly she wanted to show up, she couldn't.

Our biological mom did come the following Christmas. We visited her in her apartment with her boyfriend of the week. I remember our ride to her apartment in Claremont.

Again, my sister and I were so excited. I remember thinking how impressed she would be to see the boy that I had become. Once she saw me and got to know me, she would change her mind and want to take me back.

You must remember, for a child, the most precious relationship is to a parent. Very little, including the worst neglect and abuse, can totally dissolve the desire for a parent's approval. While we were taken away from her for good reason, it would be years before I stopped looking for her approval.

I don't remember a lot from the visit, but what I do remember ended our ability to see our mother for many years to come.

My excitement to be around my mother was some next level shit. I was absolutely out of control at her apartment. I don't remember what my sister was up to, but I know I couldn't shut up about the candy mom had bought us. I was begging and pleading with her to give us our candy. My mom was starting to get angry, and even more frustrated was her boyfriend. As a result, they believed that it would be a great idea to put me in timeout. This was done by handcuffing my arms behind my back, with real handcuffs, and placing me in the closet outside of the kitchen. I remember being in that dark closet crying, terrified for my life. I mean for fucks sake, I was a child. At that moment, I remember regretting my inquiry into wanting to get to know my mother. I wanted to go back with my adoptive parents. I don't have a solid recollection of how the remainder of the visit went, but I know that we were rescued by my adoptive parents.

My adoptive mother later explained that when they arrived at the house, they pounded on the door for almost an hour waiting for my mother and her shithead boyfriend to give us back. My adoptive mother confessed that she felt uneasy when dropping us off, and that she and my adoptive father drove around with an unsettled feeling the duration of our visit.

I was told that after about an hour, my mother answered

the door and let me out of the closet. My adoptive mother stated that I ran out of the house screaming and crying and hid behind them while the boyfriend grabbed my sister from inside and threw her down the stairs. My sister has Cerebral Palsy and had just had surgery on her legs and was in casts. Needless to say, we didn't see my biological mother again for at least five or six years. My rage and hatred towards the world intensified greatly. I started punching holes in the wall at home, swearing, and stealing daily. I rarely followed the rules and guidelines set by my adoptive parents. I did not care anymore, and I'm sure that was evident by my behavior.

CHAPTER SIX

TRAITS OF A SERIAL KILLER

Why do I feel so incomplete
Am I destined to fall to this defeat
Spirits of darkness arise from within
Why is it so comfortable every time I sin?

After the visit with our biological mother, it was decided that it would be best to enroll my sister and I back into counseling. As usual, this also included some new diagnosis and a host of medications. As a child, I often refused my medications. They always made me feel strange and different. Different, of course being the root of strange. This meant that I would be seeing a new counselor. This was a common occurrence, as I seemed to go through counselors like toilet paper. My new counselor was a man named Fred. I'd had many counselors through the years, but Fred was different. Our client patient relationship lasted for several years. I would go each week and drink hot cocoa and play chess. I didn't beat him until our final session; I'm still convinced that he allowed me to win.

At the heart of these visits were conversations surrounding my behavior. My parents used to go in and visit with Fred before I did. They would tell him all the terrible endeavors I had engaged in that week. Looking back, it was necessary because from the ages of nine to twelve, I really started to spiral out of control. I was assaulting people, throwing furniture, killing frogs from the pond by my house and setting fires. Setting fires excited me beyond belief—the experience of spreading gas or some other accelerant around, knowing that as soon as you put a flame to it there would be the wonder of how much damage it would do. Read that last line again. This is a metaphor, although it makes sense here in this paragraph, it will make more sense later in this story.

My attitude moving forward was one of rage which fueled the motto I lived by which was, "The world owes me, and I'm going to take mine." I took and took but never felt as if I could get or have enough, seeking contentment but continually finding more and more dissatisfaction.

In 1992, my adoptive mother became pregnant. Due to infatuation with myself and my quest to find some relief from my internal suffering, I was oblivious to what this would do to the attention that I was constantly seeking from my adoptive parents. A few months into her pregnancy, my adoptive mother caught my adoptive father cheating on her — second time, same woman. I remember a pretty heated argument resulting in him leaving. During the argument, my adoptive father said he would not come back as long as I was still living there. This crippled me. I folded up on the inside. Everyone who stated they love me leaves. What the hell is wrong with me? Am I such a bad person? He did end up coming back right before my new little brother was born in February of '93. I clearly remember the day my brother was born. More importantly than that, I remember the excitement of finding out that my adoptive father was moving back in.

Shortly after my celebration of having my family back, my adoptive parents split up again. My adoptive mother was now working full-time and trying to raise a new baby. I remember her being super upset one evening, and my adoptive father was not there. I asked what was wrong, and she angrily stated that my adoptive father had continued to cheat on her. That bastard! "How could he do this to me?" was all I could think. I asked what was going to happen to me. My adoptive mother stated, "No matter what happens I am always going to be here for you. I'm not going anywhere, and neither are you." I really wanted to believe her, but based on past experiences I was unable to do so. This conversation was the start of a downward slide to which I am grateful every day I came out of alive. With my adoptive father gone I lacked supervision after school until my adoptive mother got out of work at night. This meant as soon as I got off the bus after school, I would get into as much mischief as humanly possible.

The year was 1996, and I was 13 years old. I went outside to "play." My play at the time is not something you would see on television or view out your kitchen window. I was on a mission to cause destruction, with the intention to subdue some of my internal suffering. I headed down to the shed that was behind our house. It provided enough cover to hide my mischief from unwanted attention. An idea had struck me on my way down that I should fill my plastic winter sled with accelerant and set it on fire. I did just that and then laid down a trail of accelerant heading to the sled. When I lit it, there was a massive explosion. It set several items surrounding the shed on fire, including the side of the shed itself. There was this overwhelming sense of fear that the shed was going to burn down, or I would set the forest on fire. I loved this feeling and welcomed it. I was able to throw buckets of water on the shed to put that out and attempted to hide the rest of the damage. When I felt complete, I ran inside to pretend as if nothing had happened. I was scared of what had just happened but became accustomed to these feelings and enjoyed the thrill of whether or not I would get away with it.

Later that evening, the police came to the house. My grandmother had been mowing our back yard and discovered what I had done. The police officer stated that I was in trouble. This was not a new interaction for me as my adoptive father had caught me stealing several times and for some reason always found it necessary to bring me to the cops. The officer stated that he would be calling my adoptive mother to discuss how to handle the situation. Later that night my adoptive mother came home from work. She seemed mortified with what I had done. Here I was thinking it was magical. She stated she was calling my counselor Fred to set up an emergency meeting. I was unsure of whether or not I was supposed to be nervous, but I wasn't. I was excited to see my counselor again; after all he was the only one that seemed to understand what was going on with me.

Later that week, we went in for an "emergency" appointment with Fred. Although divorced, my adoptive parents were both still heavily involved with my therapy. They went in before me, which was normal, but this time they stayed in there an unusually long amount of time. Finally, the door opened, and Fred came out to the lobby and asked me to come into his office. He didn't seem to possess the same excitement to see me that he normally did. My parents were still in the room, and I asked why that was the case. I was a cocky little shit with a "get away from me" attitude written all over my face everywhere I went. Fred stated that my actions had forced my adoptive parents to make a very difficult decision. He stated that he had recommended months ago that they file a C.H.I.N.'s petition on me. "What the hell is a C.H.I.N.'s petition?" I asked. Fred stated that I would be going to a group home where I could receive the help I needed. I stated, "Yeah right, I'm not going anywhere." He said that I had a court date in two weeks, and at that time I would more than likely go directly there after leaving the court. After our meeting I didn't give the court date much thought at all. I continued acting and doing how and what I wanted.

The court date rolled around, which happened to conveniently take place on the last day of seventh grade. My adoptive father stated the night before this date that he would be waking up at nine a.m. to bring me to court. I disregarded his demand and got on the bus and headed to school. Around nine a.m. I was called down to the principal's office. Having been suspended from school several times, I was no stranger to the principal's office. Apparently, it is not okay to throw a stapler off the 4th story balcony, or pour a bottle of Tabasco sauce into your teacher's coffee, or shoot tacks at your classmates. These kinds of behaviors were not tolerated and led to numerous suspensions from school.

As I was walking down to the office, I couldn't think of why I was making this trip. Which was common. Usually when I was called down to the office I had such a long list of things that it could be for, I wasn't able to pinpoint just one. Today was different. I hadn't done anything at all (that I could recollect). Of course, it was the last day of school, so it could have been for anything. When I approached the office, my adoptive father was standing there. He looked at me and said, "Let's go, you are late for your court hearing." I told him I wasn't going and pleaded with him to not make me. He grabbed me by the arm and nearly dragged me out to his car. The result of that story is that I was shipped to Jefferson, NH, which is in the middle of nowhere. I remember arriving there and not really understanding what was happening to me. This was not unusual, as I felt this way every day.

—CHAPTER SEVEN—

PACKED BAGS

Frustrating himself
With thoughts of pure evil
Over powering all that's right
Absolute hatred and hostility
So unbearable

When my adoptive parents drove away I started to think, "Oh this is it—it is happening again." Were they leaving me like everyone else who had ever said they loved me? Was I so out of control that no one wanted me? Half of that was true; I was absolutely out of control. I proved this by launching a chair across the room upon my arrival at this group home. This seemed like a normal occurrence here because the staff and my peers didn't even bat an eye. This was the first of many attempts at "rehabilitation." Rehabilitation is still a word that I have yet to find the meaning of. I was anything but rehabilitated at this group home, or the two that followed. What I learned at these places was a host of compounding and accelerating behaviors and adaptations that allowed me to hide from and get relief from my internal suffering.

In the year that I was a ward of the state, my internal dialogue really started to fire on all cylinders. I began to reflect on the meaning of life, to really contemplate my existence. The lie that started to expand in my thoughts was that of how everyone that had ever stated they loved me had abandoned me. They left, walked away, stated they were disappointed in me. I questioned whether my life held any meaning at all. Many nights I would lie awake in bed and ponder thoughts regarding whether anyone would miss me if I weren't here. Would anyone even acknowledge my disappearance? It was starting to sound like an easy solution to the daily internal dialog within my mind.

My roommate in the second group home was a kid named Ben. Ben was so cool. He was constantly getting away with mischievous behaviors that I always seemed to get disciplined for. Ben started to educate me about sex, drugs, and rock and roll. We would often stay up late listening to inappropriate music Ben had snuck in from visits home and discussing the fuckery that the world had cast upon us. When he was talking, I was his student. He talked about how much pot he smoked before being trapped in this place, and how he was smoking on his visits and passing his drug tests when he came back to our little home away from home.

I knew of pot due to my biological father smoking it on the couple of visits that I'd had with him. In that setting, it was not attractive to me at all. My biological father's life was nothing that I ever wanted. I had subconsciously decided in my youth to avoid any actions that could possibly lead to me living the life of my biological father. Even the few times that my adoptive parents let me visit with him as a child, I never felt connected to him. It was almost as if I had withdrawn from the idea of knowing him. I never understood my resistance towards him, especially contrasted to my insistent yearning to know, and have my mother in my life. But, when Ben talked about smoking pot, it appeared to be what I had been missing all along. The pure joy and excitement that would take over his entire being when he discussed it allowed me to possess a sense of relief. I could not wait to try this magical medicine. I used to hound Ben to bring a sample for me from one of his visits back home. Every visit he stated he would, but every return was a letdown.

Behind the house where we were being held against our will, Ben and I would go sledding and hide in the woods smoking cigarettes and launching snowballs at passing cars. He snuck an album back in from a visit that absolutely changed my life. The album was "40 Oz's to Freedom" by a band named Sublime. The first time he played it, I felt as if I was being carried away. Bradley, the lead singer and author of all the magical words that filled the poetry in every song got me. It was if he understood what had been going on in my head. What I didn't know was that one of my favorite songs off this album was written regarding Bradley's struggles with heroin addiction. This would become clearer to me later on in my life.

One of the strongest memories I had about this placement—outside of the fact that my adoptive mother hated the place—was the fact that every single Friday my adoptive father would pick me up and drive me back home. Every Friday he would pick me up and buy me a soda and chips. It was the greatest feeling of all time. Finally, I was waiting for a parent who actually showed up when they said they would.

Ben ended up going back home before I did, but his influence on me lasted for many years. A couple of weeks after Ben left, I had a court date. Court dates had become so common for me that I didn't think anything of it. It usually meant that the judge would lecture me on my behavior and send me back to the facility I was at or plan my trip to the next facility. This day was different—I was about to be sprung, set free. My adoptive mother made an argument in court for my return home. She stated that I had already missed half a year of high school and should integrate back into society. The judge agreed and released me back home that day. My overwhelming excitement wasn't for going home necessarily. The excitement was to be afforded the opportunity to experience all the glory that Ben had spent countless hours prophesizing about.

I remember having a couple of weeks before school started back up. I found a job washing dishes at a local truck stop, as my adoptive mother required that I get a job since she was gone all day at work. A couple of weeks before school started, I hounded my adoptive mother to take me to the Polo outlet so I could wear the clothes that all the "cool" kids were wearing in my group homes. She obliged my request and spent hundreds of dollars on clothing for my new start. I really wanted to do well in school this time. I liked school. I mainly enjoyed literature and philosophy. I thoroughly enjoyed reading and writing. It was unclear to me at the time, but both of these tasks took me out of the torture chamber within my mind. I thought that by dressing nicer and gelling my hair, it would completely transform the lost little boy within. What I didn't know at the time was that this attempt was similar to the metaphor of polishing a turd. Yes, you can polish a turd and make it shine real nice, but it still smells like shit.

My first day back at school was not what I had made it out to be in my mind. Before homeroom had concluded, I learned that my classmates had voted on a nickname for me before I went away. That nickname was "the psycho." Although it was entirely accurate based on the behaviors that I often displayed, it crumbled my very existence. By lunch I had started to identify the kids that may have access to and potentially sell me a bag of weed. James (my old BFF, you know, the one I stole the Ninja Turtle from) and I started talking during science class. He asked me all about my "vacation," and I anxiously told him about all that I had learned. James stated that he had a bag of weed and asked if I wanted to go to his house to try it out after school. I remember thinking, that I would rather skip school and try this now! The rest of the day couldn't pass quick enough. I left several classes to find James in the school. I was like a creepy stalker. I looked through countless windows each period until I had him in my sights. He wasn't going to leave me. Not on my watch. I needed to experience the glory that Ben had described for hours and hours every night.

School ended, and I ran out of the school to meet James in the parking lot to walk up to his house. He invited a few other kids that I knew from before I left. All these kids used to be out of my reach as far as friendship was concerned. They were popular, and well, I was anything but. Up until then no one wanted to hang out with me because my behavior was too unpredictable. I was a loose cannon. James, the other three kids, and myself walked up to his house as if we were on a mission from God. Nothing, and I mean nothing, was going to stop me from experiencing the glory of smoking this magical plant that Ben had educated me on.

When we arrived at James' house, everyone walked out back to his father's tool shed. They seemed to know what they were doing so I followed their lead. James pulled out a bag of green stuff that smelled like a skunk's ass and put a chunk of it into a metal thing. It looked like the pipe that the caterpillar from Alice in Wonderland smoked out of. James put the device to his lips and set the green stuff on fire. He sucked it into his lungs. Within a couple seconds of his pull, he was coughing and spitting all over himself. Everyone including me started laughing hysterically. It appeared that he was going to die. His eyes glossed over and he had snot bubbles coming out of his nose. I remember thinking in this moment that despite all the hype that Ben gave this stuff, it didn't appear to be all that magical.

James passed the pipe to me, and I pretended I knew what to do. Well, it was almost as if I did. I put it to my lips, applied fire and took a pull off it as if my life depended on it. Little did I know in that moment that my very existence for the next 10+ years was going to depend on it. As the warm smoke filled my lungs, I began to gasp for air and started coughing uncontrollably. James stated that the only way to get rid of the cough was to take another pull as quick as possible, and so I did. I pulled even harder this time and coughed harder as well. My eyes grew warm and my nose started running with the same snot bubbles I witnessed with James. Then…all of a sudden, I began to experience the most overwhelmingly powerful body and mind sensation of my life up until that point. There was a sense of peace, a calmness that took control of me. My mind stopped. A heavy haze settled my thoughts, and in that moment, I couldn't even recall anything. It was glorious. Just as Ben had stated it would be. The rest of the evening was hazy to say the least. I remember going in James' house and eating snacks until we felt sick to our stomachs. For the first time in my life, I felt like everything was going to be okay. Everything was exactly how it was supposed to be. The thing that I didn't take into account was that it wasn't going to stay that way.

The effects of the pot wore off a couple of hours after returning home. I immediately phoned James and asked if he could get me a bag of weed. He stated he could, and I could grab it from him tomorrow at school. I was so excited — my very own bag of weed! Ben would be so proud of me. From that day forward, my high school career consisted of having and/or being around those who had weed. My friends became all the kids that I vowed to never hang around due to their resemblance to my biological father. None of that mattered. The cost of association was outweighed by the amazing and enchanting effect produced. I began smoking weed every day, all day. I started skipping school if I didn't have it so that I could find it. My grades slipped but that was not a concern to me. The only things that mattered at that point were having a job so that I could buy more weed and smoking to release my mind.

CHAPTER EIGHT

DEFINING OBSESSION

Touching the blade
Feeling the thrust
Penetrating the skin
Breaking all trust

I had been in many relationships with women at this point in my life, but nothing meaningful. There was a steady yearning within each one to run before it was too late. At the time, I was unclear and unaware of why this was so, but to be honest it didn't matter. All I cared about was staying stoned every waking moment of my existence. After work one night, I was hanging out with some kids from the grocery store where I worked. We were driving around in my car smoking weed and listening to music. One of the kids received a phone call from some girls who wanted us to go over to their house and smoke with them. We headed over. I remember that Lane, the kid that received the call, had a crush on one of them. When we pulled up to the house and the girls ran out to my car, I remember being engulfed with fear. This one girl stood out from the other two. Her name was Karen, and she was amazingly beautiful and made me stumble over my words. I was in love. I had an immediate need to have her in my life. Unknown to me at the time was the fact that this was Lane's crush. I'm not sure it would have mattered if I did know.

We smoked, laughed and talked. I fell deeper in love with Karen. She was so intelligent and beautiful. Although she was kind of sloppy from drinking wine she had stolen from her father, she made my heart skip. It's as if time stopped when I was in her presence. We left after a few hours. I ended up getting her phone number before we left that night. Lane wouldn't shut up about all the things he was plotting to do to Karen sexually. He went on and on. Clearly, he was blind to the fact that I had fallen in love with Karen and was going to make her mine.

I called Karen the following day to see if she wanted to go out on a date. She stated that she did. She asked me if I had any weed. I made her aware of the fact that I sold weed, and therefore never did not have weed. I wasn't selling it to make money, because I rarely did, except when I ripped off some younger kids. I picked her up, and we went down to my favorite spot by my house. It was a private beach on Mascoma Lake. That beach still holds a special place in my heart due to all the family functions that had been held there over the years. Our date consisted of smoking a ton of weed and fooling around in my back seat. We stayed there for hours. I drove Karen back to her house and upon leaving, I felt this weird sensation come over me. A sensation that I did not experience again until meeting my wife 10+ years later.

I talked to my adoptive father about my experience the following morning. My relationship with my adoptive father became much stronger after the divorce. I turned to him with all my questions, as most children do with their parents. Well, everything outside of the amount of pot we smoked. That morning, he once again gave me that very crucial piece of advice: "Mark, wrap your meat, or you may get something you can't wash off in the shower." He then proceeded to the bedroom and found a box of condoms for me. He asked if I knew how to use them, and I told him I did. I had no idea how to use them, or exactly what the riddle he just shot at me meant. It didn't matter, because shortly after that conversation, Karen called me and stated that she couldn't see me anymore.

I had an instant pit in my stomach that stayed with me that entire day. My world just fell in around me. I didn't know how to respond at first. Then out of nowhere came this overwhelming hatred towards her and all women. My adoptive father used to tell me that all women were lying whores. I didn't want to believe him, but it was appearing to be accurate. All the hatred I held onto towards my biological mother came back. I remember screaming and swearing at the sky hoping that Karen would experience the worst that life had in store for her.

Karen called me the following day to tell me that she had changed her mind and wanted to hang out with me again. In a single instant, all the self-judgment I had been whirling in, and the hatred of women vanished. I asked her if she wanted to stay over at my adoptive father's with me. I told her I pitched a tent in his yard, and we could stay out back. My adoptive father argued with me regarding the plan that I had established, but I knew he would give in, and my adoptive mother would stand firm in her conviction that I was too young to have women spend the night. Karen stated that she was excited, and we set a time for me to pick her up. I will spare you the graphic details of the events that unfolded, but will state that I lost my virginity to Karen. Karen and I were inseparable from that point forward. Inseparable is kind of an understatement. Karen turned into an obsession. I craved more and more of her in an attempt to quench the thirst within. Although I was always left dehydrated.

Each day I was consumed with thoughts of what she was doing, where she would be going, who she would be hanging out with. I didn't know it at the time, but I was viewing my relationship with Karen through the lenses of the relationship I had with my biological mother. I had a deep-rooted fear that Karen would just vanish one day, without a note or an explanation. School was no longer a necessity, nor was work. I began skipping both of these and would stay at my friend Austin's house all day smoking copious amounts of weed and drinking liquor from his parents' cabinet. Austin and I began hanging out all day every day. We had so much in common. Catching a buzz consumed my life; but not just catching a buzz—reaching oblivion.

There was something about Austin that really intrigued me. It could have been his knowledge of various narcotics and the results that they would produce on the mind and body, or the fact that he had also been to group homes and had a similar childhood. Our common bond was a shared hatred for the world. Austin taught me about snorting pills, taking ecstasy, drinking liquor, assaulting people, robbing stores, and many other important life-adaptation tools that would come in handy.

It was around this time that my consumption of narcotics outweighed the amount of money I was bringing in each week from my part-time position at the grocery store. Because it was cutting into my weekend partying schedule, I ended up quitting my job. They were fed up with me anyway. I was notorious for sucking the aerosol from an entire case of whipped cream cans, going out to push carts and disappearing for an hour or two, not making my shifts on time, or at all. My life consisted of finding and consuming as many substances as I possibly could.

One day, completely out of money and without a job, I made the decision to sneak into my adoptive mother's bedroom while she was in the shower and take a little money from her purse. As I was doing this, my brother snuck up behind me and screamed to my mother in an attempt to notify her of what I was up to. I turned around to tell my brother to shut his mouth, and he screamed again. I punched him in his face and left her bedroom with the money. When my adoptive mother got out of the shower, she was furious. She stated that she knew I had been taking money from her purse, but was just waiting to catch me. She started crying, saying that she had given me anything I ever wanted, but it was never enough. She told me she knew that I had a drug problem, and I needed to leave her house.

I didn't think anything of it, as she had made this statement before, but lacked the follow through for it to become a reality for me. I drove over to Austin's house that morning in my shitty car that only had one gear due to my lack of upkeep. Because I rear-ended a car at a stoplight after nodding off while on sleeping pills, the bumper was held on by a bungee cord. The car leaked power steering fluid, but by now I was used to driving a tank. I remember I used to hammer on it to see if I could blow first gear out of it, even to taking it on the highway a few times. If you ever heard a vehicle on the highway doing 65 mph in first gear with an exhaust leak, it is a beautiful sound.

When I arrived at Austin's, I never mentioned the incident with my adoptive mother and brother. We just proceeded to do what we always did. Smoke weed, take a few shots of liquor, eat snacks, and talk shit. His parents always threw me out when they got out of work. Apparently, they were not big fans of coming home to find me always at their house combined with the fact that they usually couldn't see through the veil of weed smoke. Today was no different. At around 5:30 p.m. his mother returned home from work and told me to "get to steppin'"and so I did.

I headed home, completely forgetting what had happened earlier that morning. I arrived home, and within five minutes heard a pounding on the door. It was the police. I opened the door, and they stated that I needed to leave the house, that my mother had "trespassed" me from the property. I swallowed hard. I had nowhere to go, no place to call home. Instead of owning what I had done, I started cursing my adoptive mother for "what she had done to me." I quickly got a bag of belongings together and headed to my car. The police kindly made me aware of the fact that my license had been suspended for an unpaid speeding ticket so I was not to drive my vehicle.

I called my friend Todd and asked him to pick me up, explaining to him that my mother had thrown me out, and I had nowhere to go. I wasn't clear with either Todd or his parents about exactly what had gone down at my mother's. I knew that if I told them I was a thief and that my mother had finally caught me, I would not be able to stay with them.

During this time, Karen and I had broken up. Without my car, I wasn't able to drive to go see her, and apparently, she didn't think enough of our relationship to put the effort in to come see me. I didn't care anymore. I started having daily thoughts of ending it all. The hatred towards my biological parents overwhelmed me throughout each day. "They did this to me." "This is all because of them." These were common delusional states that I lived in. I had spent a majority of my life blaming others for every situation I placed myself in. I always found someone else to blame, and if you had the childhood I did, it wasn't hard to find a scapegoat. Playing the victim was a position I stood in for many years. I could easily get others to feel bad for me and my situation. I had so much practice using lies and manipulation to show others just how the world had wronged me. It was easy, until I had burned every bridge leading anywhere in life.

CHAPTER NINE

HOW MANY BOTTOMS ARE THERE TO HIT?

I remember a time when I could stay afloat
Thought I would be doing the world a favor if I slit my own throat
Perfect planning on my part I've just written the introduction to
my suicide note
Wait that's not what I'm trying to say...

Todd's parents treated me like their own son. They fed me, clothed me, and made sure I got to school on time. One of the bonuses of living at Todd's was that his older brother sold pot. I was always helping myself to his stash. One night we had a party out on Todd's land and invited a ton of people. Per usual, at these functions, I ended up getting black-out drunk. I don't remember much of the night other than Karen and a couple of her friends, who I referred to as the "ho train," were there.

I woke up on a strange bathroom floor covered in puke and with a massive headache. I managed to lift myself up to look in the mirror. My face was black and blue and covered in blood. Someone heard me rustling around in the bathroom and came to check on me. It was Karen. She looked mortified. "What the fuck happened?" I asked. She stated, "You got in a fist fight with Todd's brother and wouldn't stop, so he ended up snapping a tree branch across your face." I felt it. It had to have been a thick one. I reached in my pockets to see what party favors I may have and found a pocket full of weed. I was not sure where it came from, nor did I care. I always woke up with pockets full of other people's stuff. This was a game I played at parties. I liked to see how much I could steal from others.

Karen kindly drove me back to Todd's house. I was surprised to find his mother and father greeting me at the door. They had all my belongings packed and out on the porch. They said that I could no longer stay there and that

I had been nothing but a problem since I moved in. Karen, feeling bad for me, invited me to stay at their house. We started "dating" again. I viewed it as a place to live, which included sex and food. I hadn't drawn a sober breath in well over a year at this point. I was consuming whatever I could get my hands on, whether I bought it or stole it. At this point, with only one week until graduation, I dropped out of school. My teachers stated that I would graduate if I just showed up. Well I couldn't do that. I just wanted to end it all. I began obsessing about taking my life. Karen would go to school, and I would wheel and deal all day to make sure we could get high when she got out of school. That was my job, and one I excelled at.

I started stealing from Karen's family—whether it was money off the counter, that was placed there for her brother's lunch money, or money out of a stash spot her father kept in his bedroom. This lasted for quite some time. They never said anything to me, which I enjoyed. One day I called a kid who I frequently bought weed from. He stated that he didn't have any weed at the moment, but did have something better than weed. He had me at "better than."

The combination of weed and alcohol really took me outside of my mind, and even at barely 18 years old I was fully addicted. I couldn't stop or moderate even though I had tried on several occasions. I asked him what he had, and he said he would pick me up in an hour. Back at his house, he pulled out a stack of little wax baggies containing some brown powder. I had no idea what it was, but was curious to know what the hype was about. He stated that sniffing one of these baggies was the equivalent of smoking a blunt.

"Well I might as well smoke two blunts then. What's that going to cost me?"

"$10 per bag," he replied.

"I'll take two then."

I cut open the two bags of powder I had just purchased and poured them on the top of the glass coffee table. I snorted them in one massive line. I remember the feeling as if it was yesterday. Within a couple of minutes my body was tingling, my eyes slanted, and my mind stopped racing. It was the most amazingly euphoric feeling I had ever experienced. I asked what I had just done, something a normal person probably would have done in the beginning. He replied, "Heroin."

Oh my God! I thought to myself, I was never going to do that. Only junkies did that stuff. Losers like my biological parents. Those thoughts lasted only a moment or two, and I settled back into the amazing feeling that was heroin. The kid drove me back to Karen's house. A couple of minutes into the short ride back, I asked him to pull over, as I was about to get sick. He jerked his car over as if he had done this 1,000 times before, and I jumped out, oblivious to all those around me. I sat cross-legged puking my brains out. It felt so good. When I got done, I felt as if I was even more intoxicated than I was before I got sick. He dropped me off back at Karen's, and I called him every day, multiple times per day, to get more and more of that magical drug. I even cut down on smoking weed. Why did I need weed now? This was definitely better than weed.

When Karen's parents had enough, they called the mom of one of Karen's friends, and I went to stay with them. I stayed with them until I stole a debit card and withdrew a few hundred dollars from their account. They asked me to leave, as everyone else had. I was a loser, and I knew it. I was an addict, but I was less willing to admit that.

I couch surfed around the area, staying in a half-dozen places, none of which lasted that long. I continued to steal from and fight with people. I was absolutely out of control. I was on a suicide mission. I had thought about dying so many times, but couldn't seem to muster up the courage to do it myself. I figured one of these nights of being under the influence would be my last. At this time, I had acquired a job working for a packing and moving company, if you call it working. I was constantly stealing from the place, selling packing boxes people and not ringing them up. I was taking money from people and giving them a truck to rent without putting it in the register, or ever filling out the proper paperwork. My life was pitiful, although it felt normal. I really imagined everyone on earth going through the same daily struggles.

I went into work one day, but this day was different. I had nowhere to go after work. I had a phone with all kinds of numbers programmed in, but knew that none of the individuals in there would pick up if they saw my number come up. This is the place in which many reach their "bottom." One man's "bottom" always seemed to be an even greater reason for me to get loaded. I stole the entire deposit from that night's business transactions and walked out with zero intentions of ever going back. After leaving, I walked around the city hoping to see anyone that might have a substance that would relieve me from the way in which I felt inside. My mind was racing with every car that passed, I became riddled with fear, as I didn't know who was behind the wheel or in the car.

At this point, I didn't have a single friend. Multiple people wanted to hurt me for the actions I had taken against them or someone that they knew. This is a cleaned-up way of saying I had fucked over every single person in my life and was known all over the area as a scumbag: a reputation rightfully deserved.

I was able to get my hands on a couple of 40 oz bottles of booze and a handful of pills. After the first 40 oz was down the hatch and the Xanax kicked in, the morbid thoughts dissipated. I had forgotten that I had just taken $900 from my job and the rest of the world wanted me dead. I began to think about my next options. Without much effort, I remembered that I did have one friend left. Austin! I hadn't talked with him in several weeks, but nonetheless I called him. The explanation of how I was down on my luck and walking the streets was a common story, and there wasn't much difficulty on my end getting it out to others. Austin stated that I could come live with him and his girlfriend until I got on my feet again. I was 19 years old and had one friend left. Austin was the only person in my life that I hadn't burned, at least that I could remember. Austin came and picked me up. When I got

Mark Crandall

in the car with him, i
gave him a couple of
a couple of joints on t.

While I lived
daughter, he got me a
Once again, the money
required for me to stay
local gas station. Austii
to steal alcohol and othe
going for a bit. I was fir
in late and under the infl
minimum wage anyway
my relationship with Aus
talking much on a day-tc
would take off all the tim

from you." That line had been
even say it with conviction
his PlayStation and some
the money to replace
sister-in-law's rent
somewhere and
be my last. Y
would ke
cousin
fatl

...c in the middle of
nowhere. I was drunk all the time and couldn't get out of my
own way most days.

One day I was completely out of money and had
nothing to take me out of my head. The stores in the area
were catching on to the fact that I never spent any money,
but went in several times per day. It was too risky to steal
anything. I started rummaging through the house. The long
and the short of it is I ended up finding $550 in a cereal box.
Not knowing what this was or whom it belonged to, I took
it. I immediately bought some booze and a pack of smokes.
Then I got some pills. This was the most devastating point
in my run with substances. I didn't get any relief. I drank a
12-pack, ate a handful of pills, and smoked two pretty good-
sized joints. Still, I could not stop thinking about how I had
just stolen from my only friend.

It was a couple of days before anyone noticed that
the money was gone. Of course, there was the usual chaos
surrounding things that I stole.

"Where did it go?"

"You didn't take it?"

"It was just here, and you were the only one home."

My defense was always the same, "I would never steal

sed so many times I couldn't
any longer. Austin had to pawn
other belongings to come up with
what I had stolen. Turns out it was his
money. I just wanted to crawl into a hole
die. Each day I woke up hoping that it would
et each day I would end up catching a buzz that
ep me until the following day. Around this time my
Freddy came into the picture. This was my adoptive
er's nephew. He had me come stay with him a couple of
towns over.

Freddy came to pick me up at Austin's. I had a couple of bags packed and was on the porch ready to go. Austin didn't even say goodbye to me, nor did I make eye contact with him. Austin's girlfriend was working at the store so I decided to stop in and get one final take. This take was a little advanced from the rest. I decided to take around 10 cartons of cigarettes and several cases of beer, so much stuff that I had to make a couple of trips back to Freddy's car. Oh, and a case of Slim Jims. I always took Slim Jims for some odd reason. This seemed to be my trademark. When we arrived at Freddy's house, I quickly learned that he had three other roommates. Although I was thrilled to have a place to stay, Freddy's roommates didn't appear to share my excitement...until I offered up my stolen goods. Then everyone became much more hospitable. I slept in the living room for four months, but paid no rent and contributed nothing at all. This was my first bottom. The lowest of lows, so I thought.

During this period, I was drinking cheap vodka daily, bottle after bottle. I ended up getting hired by a painting company that I had worked for a few years prior. I lasted for about a month. There appeared to be some promise once I got a job. Most days I would arrive at the shop unable to walk in a straight line. This didn't bother them at all, they just were not going to let me drive a company van. The end of the end came on my last Friday painting. I hadn't eaten in days due to not having any money. I came back to Freddy's house angry as all hell. I had been drinking all afternoon at work and taken some pills and smoked a truck full of weed. I started drinking vodka like it was the last bit of air on earth. I have vivid memories of blasting "Sober" by Tool in the basement. It was on repeat, and I couldn't stop crying and kicking and punching holes in the wall. I wanted to die, and if I had had access to a gun in that moment, I more than likely wouldn't be sharing this account today.

When I woke up in the morning, Freddy and his roommates confronted me. They stated that I had a problem, and I had better get help. I was stunned and completely puzzled by their statements. I needed help? These dirty hippies are in the same state as I was. This offended me. I need help…Not even sure what the hell that means. They then told me I was no longer allowed to stay with them. Then it hit me. Here I was again, same place as always. Ever since birth:

People giving up on me.

People throwing me away.

People tossing me out with the trash.

I couldn't think of anyone to call at this point. It was over. Maybe I should just jump off a cliff. No one would miss me if I did. I had a thought that was not of me. It was as if a guiding force passed me a note that read "Dear Shithead, call your Grandparents (Oma and Opa — German for Grandmother and Grandfather, my biological father's parents), they will help you." I wasn't sure it would work but I was willing to give it a shot.

I picked up the phone and called my Oma and Opa. Opa answered the phone with excitement. It was almost as if they were expecting my call. This was the first time I had authentically asked for help. It wasn't a place to stay, but genuine help. "Opa I'm in a bad way, I have nowhere to go and don't even want to live any longer." Without hesitation, he asked where I was and came to pick me up.

CHAPTER TEN

CRY FOR HELP

I am but a man;
Withered with decay.
I am but a man;
Who survived another day.

When I arrived, my Oma had a dismal look on her face. She appeared to be distraught and disappointed. She told me to go get cleaned up for dinner. In that moment, I felt a glimmer of hope. Although it was short lived, it was enough to keep me from taking my life. I agreed to refrain from using any and all drugs while I lived with them. I eagerly agreed, although unaware of the fact that this wasn't a possibility. I was however allowed to drink beer while I lived there.

Two days into living there, Opa wanted to go hiking. I wasn't a big adventure guy, but the plan was to pick up some beers and go hiking. Anything that had to do with beers sounded like a good time to me. I remember drinking way too many beers. My backpack was full when we left and empty before we got to the top. When I got home, Oma just shook her head and said, "Before dinner Mark? What is wrong with you?" I didn't know the answer to that riddle. I just knew that I felt so hollow inside all the time and the only relief I had ever found was through ingesting alcohol and other substances. I was also starting to figure out that no matter how many or how much I intended on having, I always overshot that. Usually there had to be some separation from the alcohol or substances for me to stop. Generally, an intervention by someone or something was required as I was unable to stop on my own once I took any mind or mood-altering substance into my system.

I managed to get two jobs while living at Oma and Opa's house, one of which was sanding drywall for a large construction company. I enjoyed this job because it afforded me an environment to drink and do as many drugs as I wanted as long as I could get my tasks done. I was provided two raises in pay while there for my hard work. I also took on a job at a local pizza place making pizzas after I got out of my drywall job. My Oma was budgeting my money for me, buying my smokes and giving me spending cash each week. She learned after the first paycheck that I did not possess the skills to do that on my own, and she surely didn't want me living with her forever.

Probably a month into living with my grandparents I was having some severe tooth pain. This wasn't a surprise, as I hadn't seen a dentist in years. My Oma made me an appointment to see a dentist and I went to see them. They were unable to do anything on me that day, as the infection in my mouth was too bad to be worked on. They sent me home with antibiotics and pain medicine. I didn't know it at the time but this visit was going to be the beginning of the darkest life I have known to date. The dentist that wrote my prescription wrote me a prescription for 30, 10mg Vicodin with five refills. The refills were not supposed to be on there, but I wasn't going to say anything. I hadn't done an opiate in months, but when I filled that prescription and threw two into my mouth, that feeling returned. Everything disappeared. I felt alive, like I could do anything. However, I wasn't capable of doing anything. As I filled those prescriptions just as quickly as they were available at the pharmacy my life blurred by. Along with all responsibilities or care for life.

I had been "sober" now for three months, drinking and eating my Vicodins. Things were going well. I wasn't partying or hanging out with bad influences; in fact, I wasn't hanging out with anyone. My spare time consisted of drinking beers and playing video games in the basement of my grandparents' home. One Saturday afternoon my cellphone rang. I didn't know the number, but I picked up. It was Austin. He wanted to know if I wanted to go to a birthday party with him. I screamed through the phone with excitement, "YES." I was dying to get out of the house. He picked me up and immediately asked me if I wanted to smoke. I explained to him that I had made an agreement with my grandparents, and I didn't want to disobey them. We arrived at the party, and the beers were flowing. I was pounding them. The combination of the pills I had taken that morning and the beer had me in a full wobble by noon.

On the ride back to my grandparents', I told Austin to pass the weed. I smoked a couple of bowls, but before the second bowl ended, I made the decision that we needed to buy a bag for me to take home. My Oma had found me an apartment to go look at. She never said it to me but I was beginning to feel as if I was a burden on her and my Opa. My Opa brought me to look at the apartment, paid the deposit and made plans for me to move in. I did not have any say in the matter. My Opa decided this was the place I needed to live, and I was moving in the following week, not that I cared much either way.

Austin came the following weekend and helped me move into my new apartment. Once we had all the furniture and all the things my Grandmother had gathered up for me we proceeded to get wasted. I was on my own for the first time ever. Quickly I learned that I had no idea how to live on my own. Nothing mattered as long as I had what I needed to feel okay on the inside. Unfortunately, my prescriptions ran out. I quickly learned where to get more. There was a woman down the street that seemed to always have what I needed. I only knew her by her street name, Grasshopper.

When I first met Grasshopper, she seemed like a sweet woman. She always invited me inside and wanted to know what was going on with me. It was never a chew and screw with her. There was always good conversation. A couple of days into my frequent visits she ran out of pills. I was devastated. She stated, "I have something better if you're interested." I had heard this same phrase before, but was unclear where. Without a second thought I said, "You have some heroin?" I was so excited. I literally felt as if I was high before I had even made the purchase. Visiting Grasshopper became a multiple day occurrence. Before I knew it, the money my Oma had saved for me was gone, and I was living paycheck to paycheck. I started stealing from co-workers—money out of their lockers or drugs out of their vehicles. It didn't take long for them to identify who the common denominator was. I was quickly the outcast at the shop. No one would smoke with me on breaks or talk with me throughout the day. This didn't affect me, as long as I could stay under the influence. Nothing mattered to me when I had my fix.

One day on lunch break I was getting stoned when all of a sudden my back went out. I collapsed to my knees. Confused and scared I tried to stand up, but was unable to do so. What the hell was happening to me? I'm only 21 years old at this point. Terrified I called my Opa and explained to him what was happening. He told me to leave work and go to the hospital. I listened to him and did just that. I couldn't straighten my back and was in a great deal of pain. The hospital ran a bunch of scans and tests on me. The doctor asked what I did for work and I explained that I sanded drywall with a portable sander and that the majority of the work I did was overhead, meaning I had to sand the ceiling joints on the houses we assembled in the shop. Because this happened at work they explained to me that it would be a workman's comp case. I didn't know what that meant. All I heard from that visit was that I was going to be prescribed Percocet for the pain.

Percocets quickly turned into Oxycontin and Fentanyl patches. I was unable to work during this period. I honestly couldn't tell you how much of it was back pain or just a desire to stay within the story I had created to continue to get my medications. My money dwindled as I waited for the workman's comp checks to come in. My apartment went from a clean place I called home to a disgusting flop house where all the misfits could party. It was gross! Trash was everywhere; a pile of dishes hadn't been cleaned in months; and a smell that gallons of bleach couldn't counter permeated the air.

Eulogy Of Childhood Memories

Because of my overwhelming need to buy drugs and alcohol, I fell behind on rent. Each week when the landlord showed up, I would hide. The Sheriff's office served me an eviction notice, and I stayed in that apartment until the last day of the notice. I was forced to sell my medications to survive, as I had no other income. My existence was completely hollow. I only went outside at night out of fear that I would be assaulted by one of the countless people I had ripped off. I hated myself, hated the very thought of continuing to live this way. And yet, those thoughts disappeared once I got high.

I moved in with some girls who lived across the street from me. Of course, the agreement we made was that I would pay them once my checks came in, and in the mean time I gave them pills from my prescriptions as I filled them. Although I won the workers' comp claim, I was trading most of my medications for heroin, and my life was completely unmanageable. I missed my final date, which was created to agree on a settlement for my injury. This was likely a blessing as the amount being discussed would probably have been enough to kill me.

I did receive two paychecks for lost wages of around $3,000. I remember the Friday that they came in. I quickly ran to the bank to cash them. It happened to be the same day that my prescriptions were refilled. This was glorious as I had the money to fill them on my own for the first time. Which in drug addict terms meant that I could keep all my medication to abuse at my leisure. I filled my prescriptions and went to the liquor store and to meet one of my heroin dealers. I had done a bunch of Oxy's that day and had been drinking since noon. When I arrived at the dealer's house I traded him some Oxy's and cash for a large amount of heroin. I snorted three bags and got ready to leave his house. As soon as I got outside my breathing became constricted. I had to get down on one knee. I remember saying a prayer, "Please God don't take me yet." The meaning of the prayer had nothing to do with any life I felt I had yet to live, but everything to do with the drugs and alcohol I had yet to consume. What a life I was living.

I made it back to the apartment. I gave the girls I lived with some rent money, and we proceeded to party. I felt on top of the world, although looking back on it, my life was a complete shit show. I had become the person I stated I would never be, I would ever be anything like my biological parents. I never wanted to live paycheck to paycheck or live each day for the buzz I would acquire. It didn't take long before my money ran out. I started robbing everyone I came into contact with. I was crawling through windows, waiting for people to go to work, kicking doors in, pry-barring businesses. It got dark quickly. I was again constantly looking over my shoulder. I didn't want this life. I had so much potential.

The girls I was living with asked me to leave after becoming a few weeks behind on rent and one of the girls "losing" her portion of the rent money. It wasn't lost, I had stolen it one day while she was at work. I ended up finding a homeless shelter to stay for a bit until I figured things out. I stayed there for a few weeks and was forced to see a substance abuse counselor. I had no idea what he talked to me about as I was wasted during every visit. I do know that the police were constantly there looking for me. I was always in question about crimes that had been committed. I always had an answer, I always seemed to know what to say—not that they believed me.

— CHAPTER ELEVEN —

PURSUING SOBRIETY IN OHIO

Horrified by reality
Consumed by addiction
My life is based off my own self-affliction.

Iknew I needed to get off the heroin and alcohol, but had no idea how one accomplished that. Many days had been started with the statement of "I'm not going to get high today, I'm going to go find a job and get my shit together." It never occurred to me that this wasn't an option. Within moments, each time I made this statement, no matter how strong the conviction, I was plotting how I was going to get high ASAP; the circumstances did not matter. When the thoughts of getting high were in my mind, nothing stopped me from achieving it.

I had a phone conversation one day with my sister, who at the time lived in Ohio with her Christian boyfriend she met on the Internet. In that conversation, the idea of me going to Ohio to get sober came up. This really seemed like a million-dollar idea, as I had nowhere to go and was in question for several robberies and burglaries. I pulled off a couple of thefts and scraped together the money for a bus ticket. I ended up robbing a couple of kids the night before I left to make sure I could bring some drugs on the bus with me. Surely this is how you get sober.

My sister set clear "rules" up for me as far as what it would take for me to be able to stay with her. A few days in, I ran out of the drugs I brought with me. I came up with the idea of going to the doctor to get some medication for my back. This had worked time and time again, and worked on that day as well. I remember returning to my sister's house and walking up the street to the little pizza place to get a snack. Five or six hours later my sister and her friend and boyfriend showed up to get me to go back home. I ended up doing nearly all my prescriptions and sitting at the bar drinking myself into a black out. I don't remember much more of the night. I woke up the following morning with a return bus ticket back to New Hampshire.

My sister's boyfriend came to pick me up to take me to the bus stop. He filled me in on the nights events. Apparently, I was picking fights at the bar, and when the cops were called, I picked a fight with them. My sister called my Opa, and he was able to convince the cops to not take me to jail for who knows what. The cops ended up bringing me to a local hotel. I lucked out again. I still had some pills in my pocket and a buzz that carried over into the morning. Lord knows I needed the pills due to the shame and remorse I was feeling for the load of grief I had just caused my sister. My sister is the one person who has seen every aspect of me. She has stuck by me no matter how screwed up I was, no matter what others said about me, and no matter what I said or did to her. Here I was once again shattering the love others shared for me.

— CHAPTER TWELVE —

UP A RIVER WITH NO PADDLE TO ROW

The choices made that led to this
When the pitch came with a swing and miss
Continually making wrong decisions
Editing my life with improper revisions

When I arrived back in New Hampshire, I called Austin. He filled me in on what I had missed during the week that I was away. Several people were looking for me, including the cops. He stated that it would be best that I go into hiding. I became homeless for the next 22 days. I'd been homeless before, but not knowingly on the run from the police. The worst part is I could not remember what I was wanted for. I remember acting tough with Austin but I really wanted to curl into a ball and cry. I stayed in a cemetery that night. I balled up a hoody and used it as a pillow against a headstone. I prayed that night as I looked up to the sky and asked God to take me. Not "take me" like I offer my life to you type shit. More along the lines of if you are real, allow me to not wake up in the morning. Here I found myself on the run, an outcast to my family with a stolen cell phone filled with phone numbers of individuals that would not pick up if I called. No one wanted anything to do with me and rightly so. I was a scumbag with a raging drug habit that caused me to do things to people that I regretted, but I had no control.

I would stay awake at night shaming myself for the harm I'd caused others. There is one memory that is burned into my mind. It was the 4th of July and I had been hiding for well over two weeks. Literally, I hadn't stepped out into the light of day. I had the bright idea to go to my hometown to watch the fireworks display and catch up with a couple of buddies. I managed to get my hands on a written prescription and so I was walking to the pharmacy to get it filled, completely oblivious to the fact that it would be closed for Independence Day and all. There I was walking down the busiest section of town as if I was an upstanding citizen.

All of a sudden I heard, "Mark. Mark, what are you doing?" A car pulled up; it was my adoptive mother and stepfather. My mother said, "Get in. Let's get some breakfast before you go away."

Curious, I asked what she meant by "Go away."

She said, "You have been on the news for the past two weeks. You are wanted for all kinds of crimes."

At that point, the panic set in and I sprinted away from my mother as fast as I possibly could. Before I knew it, I could hear multiple sirens going. It wasn't my first time running; I was a veteran at evading. I took to the tree lines so they would have difficulty spotting me. I would periodically peek out to see numerous cruisers driving by. They were everywhere! Did I kill someone? What had I done? A better question was what did they know that I had done?

There I was terrified in the woods, running for reasons unknown to me. What I mean by this is that I had done so many things that could have landed me in this situation that it was hard to pinpoint what the police knew I had done. Regardless, I wasn't going to jail tonight. I had plans of getting wasted and as my experience had shown me up until now there was nothing that was going to stop that. After a few hours of hiking through the woods I made it to my friend Phil's house. I walked up to the front door and knocked.

Phil's mother answered and said, "What are you doing here? Don't you know you are wanted, and a ton of people are looking for you?"

I stated, "No, I wasn't aware of that. Is Phil home?"

Phil came downstairs. I begged him to get me stoned, and he did. At the end of our session, he said, "I can't have you coming around here anymore. My mother said she doesn't want the cops here, and they have already come here looking for you."

I told him that I wouldn't be by any more and left.

Eulogy Of Childhood Memories

After I left his house, I headed back to the woods. What was I going to do? Where was I to go? No one wanted me around, and my adoptive mother — my one bail-out plan — had already called the police on me. The feeling was crippling. I managed to steal some alcohol and sat in the woods drinking This was the lowest spot I had been in thus far in my life. I had no idea what to do. The only option was to get as loaded as possible in an attempt to forget reality. However, getting loaded is a bigger challenge when you are hiding in the woods with police from three towns trying to incarcerate you.

I did manage to get drunk that day by walking into stores, taking a couple of pints, and hiding them in my waistband. I had some money, but I surely didn't want to spend it on alcohol. What I wanted was some narcotics and I didn't care what. It was getting late, and I could hear fireworks going off and laughter and conversation around every turn of the tree line. I had been walking all day, crying and hopeless. In the midst of my pity party, the thought crossed my mind to go back to Phil's house to see if he left any weed behind that I might be able to steal. I walked back to his house, put a ladder up to his window and climbed into his bedroom. Sure enough, I found weed and money. I took both and ran back into the woods.

I walked the tree line for a few miles to a ski jump that I had slept at before, and knew there would be zero chance of getting caught. I smoked and cried myself to sleep. I had just robbed my one remaining friend.

I woke up to the sound of children. I jumped up startled and fuzzy on what had happened the night before. The children were climbing up the ski jump and collecting firework shells from the night before. I gathered all my belongings (a bag of weed, rolling papers, a lighter and my cellphone), stuffed them into my pockets, and started to run down the ski jump. The look on the two children's faces is burned into my consciousness. These kids were terrified to see me, but not nearly as terrified as I in that moment.

I had been robbing businesses on a daily basis, trying

to survive and access substances to release me from the dark thoughts that plagued every waking moment. At this point I was staying in an apartment with some girl I met who knew I was on the run. I had been locked up in her house for 20 days and was only going out at night to rob people and businesses. I was starting to really lose my mind. I was invited to a party a couple of streets down, risky business for someone who had been on the local news and on the front page of newspapers for weeks now.

After the party, a kid I met and I decided to break into a couple of stores to see what we could find. While attempting the first burglary, a door opened. I had been caught. I had taken some mushrooms and heroin and was pretty drunk. I didn't know what time it was, or even where I was. A woman hollered out the door, "I'm calling the cops, you'd better get out of here." So we did.

I told the kid I was with that we needed to stay in the woods so we wouldn't get caught. He insisted on walking in the road. I knew it was a bad idea but I was too wasted to argue. The truth is I was tired—not like I'm ready for bed or it's time for a nap tired—I was tired of living. Everything in me wanted it all to stop.

As soon as we started walking away, the police showed up. They attempted to stop us. The officer knew me by name, as they had apparently been looking for me for weeks. In that moment, I made the decision to jump over the guardrail to a 20+ foot fall onto a rock bank and into the Connecticut River. I remember the sobering moment when I was out in the current. I thought my life was over. I couldn't swim; I could barely keep my head above the water. I kicked my shoes and pants off under water to increase buoyancy. Somehow, I made it to the other side of the river and avoided arrest.

Once to the other side of the river, I broke into a house and found clean clothes and shoes that fit, and I was off, back to the apartment complex where I had been hiding out. After more than 20 days of hiding, I was out of money and drugs again. I had rolled my ankle pretty badly during my river bout, so I decided to seek medical attention. Well, really, I was in hopes of scoring some narcotics, which I did, and much more. After being released from the ER, I hobbled on crutches into the parking lot to be met by four or five police cruisers. Before I knew it, guns were drawn, and one of the officers screamed, "If you run, we will shoot you." I was on crutches and had just received a shot of fentanyl; I wasn't running anywhere. The officer who placed handcuffs on me stated that they had been looking for me for quite some time. He also said, "I will sleep better tonight knowing that a scumbag like you is off the streets." They booked me at the station and drove me to Sullivan County Jail.

-CHAPTER THIRTEEN-

INSTITUTIONALIZED

Now I'm trapped here in prison
I'm accustomed to this cell
And all the wrong decisions
That led me back to this hell

To most people the thought of going to jail is a terrifying realization, but at this point it was comforting. I knew that I had a place to sleep and would be fed. When you live a drug-addicted crime riddled life such as I had for years, the only concern in jail is how long will I be there. I had engaged in so many criminal activities that it was hard knowing what I was actually being held for. I remember my first call home. I called my adoptive mother, as I was sure she would be the only person I knew who would answer the phone. She did. I explained to her what had happened and pleaded with her to bail me out. She refused and said, "Mark, I will not bail you out. I will finally be able to get some sleep knowing that you are safe."

This devastated me. Since early childhood, I had identified myself as a victim, so from my point of view, if you had lived the life I lived, you would have surely used drugs and robbed people as well.

In jail I read books, played cards, talked to people about crime and even gained a few drug connections to use upon leaving. I wrote poetry and sold love poems to other inmates to send to their spouses, pen pals, and family. I only got high a couple times while I was in there, but they kept me on a very high dose of anti-depressants. Even so, I was seriously depressed. Every day, I thought about ending it all. It surely seemed easier than being trapped in my mind.

Wouldn't you have been depressed? I mean, here I sat in jail after a brutal two-week detox from heroin and alcohol while sleeping on the floor next to a steel urinal in an 8' x 8' cell with two other inmates. Every day I woke up to the excitement of taking my medication and staring out the window fantasizing about when I would be able to get high again. I had destroyed any and all meaningful relationships in my life and had no one who gave half a fuck about me. Once in a while there would be a fistfight over a honey bun, or who was going to watch what show on television. For some reason, I still experienced pleasure when witnessing someone else's suffering. Somehow it allowed me to shift focus off my own shame and remorse.

I had one role in the eight-man room that I was moved to after detox. My role was the cigarette stasher; meaning I was in charge of rolling and dispensing cigarettes and hiding them so that if the Correction Officers tossed our room they would not be found. It was a risky game, but I got excited about it. It was similar to the feelings experienced when breaking into a business or robbing a house. As with any illegal act, the day comes when you get sloppy and get caught. That's exactly what happened. The COs rolled in our room and right there in the open was a cigarette I was rolling. I received 10 days in solitary confinement. If you've ever been in solitary confinement (which most civil humans have not) you know how big of a mind fuck it can be. I was allowed one pen, one pad of paper and a Bible. I read the entire Bible while in my cell and managed to write an entire collection of poems, which I printed and distributed myself a few years later — some of which are used in this book.

The first couple of days in solitary confinement, I was peaceful. I slept 15 hours per day. I read, drew pictures, wrapped a towel around my face to shield the light that was always on, took night meds and went to sleep. On the third day I couldn't sleep. I read the Bible and drew and wrote. Over the next several days, I contemplated my entire existence up until that point, which had you lived the life I had, you can imagine how painful it was. I hated myself, I wanted to die, I couldn't image how I was ever going to build a life for myself.

Eulogy Of Childhood Memories

There seemed no hope at all for someone like me. After the 10 days, I was released back into the unit I came from. Everyone was happy to see me, and even more excited that I didn't tell on the cigarette supplier.

I was in County Jail for eight months. Towards the end of my stay I started attending recovery meetings in the jail. I really wanted to not have to live a life of getting high and robbing people, but I also had zero interest in feeling the way that I did on a daily basis. Yet I had no idea how to overcome either of these. When I had my discharge date the fear and excitement was so strong I could hardly contain myself. The excitement soon wore off when I started to think about all the people that would be coming to collect upon my release. I had burned at least 100 people. Before I ended up in County, I constantly looked over my shoulders everywhere I went.

I set up a deal with one of my cellmates. He wanted me to meet his girlfriend at a grocery store to drop off some cocaine and cigarettes at the nursing home — what we called the work release location — so that it could be brought back into the jail. This was too good to be true, but I had to check it out. I agreed to do it for him. For my remaining two days people in there worshiped me. They asked me a million times a day if I was really going to do it. It's all they talked about. I didn't understand the hype; although I had done it several times, I couldn't stand cocaine. I used drugs and drank alcohol to shut my mind up, not to speed my thoughts up. The last thing I wanted was to be up all night contemplating the crappy hand I had been dealt and how I was destined to die a lonely death.

My adoptive mother and stepfather picked me up from jail the day of my release. They held a huge party for me. Everyone was so hopeful that eight months was what it took for me to turn my life around. I was hopeful as well, but skeptical. I still wanted to die, although I didn't voice that to anyone out of fear I would end up in a psych hospital. I really did want it all to stop. The following day, I drove 20 miles to meet my probation officer. He stated the ground rules and wished me high hopes. I didn't really hear a word he said. All I could think about was picking up the quarter ounce of blow and a carton of smokes with zero intentions of dropping it off at the nursing home. Why would I do that? This was the Universe handing me a gift. If you believe in signs, I was certain this was one.

I drove to the grocery store to meet this mystery girl. Sure as shit, she was working in the bakery and waiting for me to arrive. She handed me a decent chunk of cocaine and $50 to buy smokes. I thanked her and headed out of the store. I began obsessing about doing it all. The reality of me hating cocaine was pushed out of my mind by thoughts of how different it will be this time. I raced back to my mother's house to cook it. Although I didn't like it, I was a wizard at cooking it into rock. First full day out of county jail I was smoking crack in my mother's house while I was supposed to be looking for work and getting back on my feet. On my third night of being home, I was geeking out pretty good when there was a knock on the door. It was a couple of probation officers. They came in my bedroom. They knew I was high. They didn't lock me back up, which I was surprised about, and it's probably a good thing because I probably would have caught a mean ass whooping from the men that expected me to drop the cocaine off.

They gave me a list of local recovery meetings and informed me that I would need to attend a minimum of two per week. I told them that it was the first thing on my to-do list. I sold them tons of sweet promises, which deep down I really wanted to live up to. I had no idea how dark it was going to get for myself, and the people around me. Later on that week I attended a recovery meeting. It was strange. I didn't feel like I fit in at all, although I knew half of the room. I was more worried about whether or not people that I ripped off would come to one of these meetings. I ended up learning that half the room was still getting high and made a couple really good connections. I managed to get some clean time, although I'm uncertain of exactly how long I had. I think around 90 days. I lied so much I was uncertain of what the truth was anymore. I met a girl at one of the meetings, and she asked me if I could get her some pills. I figured because I was now sober and living a different life I could do it no problem. I scored her a handful of pills from an old buddy. I was going to give them to her at the meeting later on that night. Nothing ever went the way I planned.

Later that evening I started getting ready to take a shower. The thought popped into my head that I bet I could do just one of the pills. There was no follow-up thought to talk me out of it. Before I knew it, I was high. I didn't end up going to a meeting that night. I went back to get more pills, starting both the most vicious and hopefully the last run of addiction that I will experience. From that day forward, I was on a mission to die by means of an overdose. I didn't want to live any longer. This time, I could say I had tried everything. I had even tried the whole recovery-meeting thing. If only people knew how fucked up those people were, I'm sure the courts wouldn't have sent me there. Or maybe they would have. For almost a year I did not draw a sober breath.

For my monthly probation visits, I was getting urine detox kits for the first couple of times. After a couple visits I didn't care anymore. I was hoping they would lock me back up. My dishwashing and prep cook job was not affording me the opportunity to get as wasted as I needed to on a daily basis. I started stealing money from tables, dipping into the register, and robbing people and businesses at night. I was drinking all day long on top of eating Xanax, smoking copious amounts of weed and doing heroin. My adoptive mother knew something was up with me, but I don't remember her saying a word about it.

One morning I was getting ready for work, which entailed smoking a joint in my adoptive mom's minivan while drinking a pint. All of a sudden, an unmarked cruiser whipped into my driveway. As soon as they pulled down the driveway I knew I was in trouble. It was Dan my Probation Officer. In that moment, I remembered that I hadn't checked in with him in a few months. Nor had I gone to those dumb recovery meetings or the rehab I was court ordered to attend. I thought about running but I didn't feel I was sober enough to get up to the speed necessary to get away. I jumped out of the van and locked the door to it. My plan was to pretend like everything was going as it was planned. Dan asked, "Where have you been? I haven't seen you at our scheduled monthly check-ins." In that moment I experienced something strange, something unidentifiable. Honesty! I looked him dead in the eyes and said, "Dan, I can't stay sober. I thought I was going to get high once to dull the voices in my head, but once I started I couldn't stop. There is something wrong with me." Dan told me that he didn't want to lock me up, but if I wasn't in rehab by next Friday he was going to have to. Dan also explained how him not locking me up that day was a huge risk for him because he could get in trouble for it. I promised him that I would get into treatment by next Friday.

I really wanted to go to treatment, to be sober, for the pain to go away. I hated robbing people, walking around with my head to the ground because I didn't want to look anyone in the eyes. I hated constantly lying to my adoptive mother and others who loved me. I absolutely hated not being able to sleep at night even with an expensive buzz because the thoughts of all the messed-up things I had done and had been done to me would not leave my thoughts. Although I wanted to fulfill Dan's wishes, I knew there wasn't a chance in hell that I would make it to rehab. I had already made plans to go to a party that night and my brother's tree fort was full of booze and cigarettes I had stolen from a local convenience store a couple of nights prior. I was planning to sell the stolen goods to fund my partying.

I met some people after work and unloaded all my stolen goods into their car to make some money and have resources (drugs) for the party that night, I managed to get Xanax, heroin, and even some cocaine. I knew better than to drink liquor with Xanax. That was the combination that always landed me in jail, or at least in a courtroom. Yet none of those thoughts ever came into my mind while I was in the middle of it. No matter how insane of an idea it may have seemed to someone else, I always truly believed that it was going to work out. My idea that night was, "I'm going to party one more night and then go to rehab." I'm pretty sure I even told everyone at the party that I was going to rehab after this party. Regardless of my intentions, what happened was I attempted to steal from the purse of the girl who was driving me home. She threw me out of her jeep in the middle of the road.

I managed to get my hands on a massive crowbar and proceeded to pop the doors of five or six businesses. I filled a backpack with a stack of cash, cigarettes, and Slim Jims. I tripped a silent alarm and was arrested. This is according to court documents. I honestly don't remember most of the evening. What I do remember was waking up a couple days after being placed in Grafton County Jail and asking what in the hell happened. Some of the inmates, who I knew from recovery meetings, filled me in. I was mortified. I was in so much trouble. The judge told me if he saw me again, he was going to send me to prison. Dan was going to be so upset with me. The next two weeks were hell, as the detox from drugs and alcohol took hold alongside the self-hatred that filled every thought I had.

See the thing that they didn't know was that the foundation that I was given as a youth in group homes prepared me for jail and prison. Operating each day based off of a schedule that someone else provided and having zero responsibility is easy. Sure, it's not fun, but it's easy. It didn't take long after another brutal detox from drugs and alcohol for me to jump right back into my daily routine. Wake up around noon, eat, play cards, write and draw, watch TV, get night meds and then read until I fell asleep. I was constantly calling my court ordered lawyer and asking if he had any news for me. Each time he would say, "It ain't looking good kid. They are really trying to send you to prison." One of the men on my unit suggested I write a letter to this treatment center. It was a year-long rehab and he told me he knew a number of people who got out of going to prison by getting accepted there.

I wrote them a letter and sure as shit got accepted. Now I just needed my lawyer to let the court know that everything was all set—I would be going to treatment, so there was no need to pursue a prison sentence. The court saw things differently. The day of my sentencing hearing my lawyer ran up to me with excitement. He stated, "They got a sweet deal for you kid. Two to seven years in prison and successful completion of the rehab you were accepted to." I said, "I'm not taking that, that's not a deal at all." He then said, "If you don't take it you're going to do a minimum of 10 years." I said, "OK, where do I sign." After the hearing was over, I headed to New Hampshire State Prison. This happens to be the greatest blessing of my life. Not because they rehabilitated me, but because while incarcerated there, I hit what people in the recovery meetings I attended referred to as a bottom.

I admit I was a little nervous on the hour ride to the prison. I was in the back of a dark van with several other men. Most of them had been to prison before. We started swapping stories and in no time my fear drifted. Once inside, it was the same thing I had become accustomed to. Eat, play cards, write, eat, play cards, sleeping meds, go to bed, and do it all over again in the morning. I read and wrote a lot while in there. My adoptive mother would come a couple of times per month to visit me. She would talk to me about what the family was up to and what she would hope I would be up to upon release. This time incarceration was different. About two weeks into my sentence, one of my cellmates asked me what kind of medication I was prescribed. I told him I was on Welbutrin, 200 mg three times per day. He asked me if I had ever tried sniffing it. I said no, I didn't know that was an option. He shared with me how amazing it was.

That night I dropped my medication down my tucked in shirt and went back to my bunk. The same man was waiting for me. We sucked the coating off the pill and snorted it. It was the most amazing thing ever. It completely took me out of the reality of being in prison. I did this every day for each med call. Another man taught me how to catch the pill in my throat and spit it back up once safely back on the unit. This was necessary because of how serious some of the Correctional Officers took the offense of "cheeking" your medications. I would also sell and trade them for other things. I smoked weed once while in there. Horrible experience. I got loopy as hell and sat on my bunk and laughed like I was in high school again. The paranoia was too much for me. I didn't do that again. Another time I got to do some heroin. That was just how I remembered it. These "escapes" came at a high risk though—as soon as you come down you have to frantically begin to pound water to attempt to flush it out of your system to avoid pissing hot and getting a disciplinary hearing. That would only mean time in the hole and less of a chance of getting out on time.

I stayed high the entire time I was in there. Because I dropped out of high school, I was mandated to complete my G.E.D. before they would release me. That was the one and only accomplishment I had for my entire two years. I passed my G.E.D. I didn't find out until a few years later how much of an impact that would have on my life. I pretty much kept to myself in there. I didn't join a gang or get caught up in gambling. Those were two of the cardinal rules a multiple visitor (multi-time inmate) shared with me upon arrival. He said, "Kid if you want to get out on time, don't get in debt, don't join a gang, and stick to your own." I understood the first two points but had to ask what the third meant. He said, "It means stick with your own color, if it's white it's right." I followed the first two of the cardinal rules, but I talked to anyone and everyone (mainly due to the fact that I was high as a kite all the time).

One day during mail call, almost two years into my sentence, I received a letter from the rehab facility I'd been accepted to. I opened it in my room as I did with all my mail. You never want to try to read someone's mail in there;

I watched multiple fights start because of that. The letter provided me with a date for admission. I had no clue what that meant. Did it mean I was going to get out? The letter read, "We look forward to your admission on August 23, 2007." Instantly I was engulfed with fear. That's in two weeks. Two weeks from now I will be going to rehab. Here it was a little after five p.m., and all I could think about was going to get and sniff my seven p.m. meds. This was it, the bottom, and the absolute lowest imaginable point of my existence. To those of you reading this it may not seem as bad as some of the other spots I was in earlier in my story, but this was the curtain for me. Someone addicted to drugs and alcohol at the level I was hardly ever reached a circumstantial bottom. I have witnessed countless individuals that have gotten a DWI and sobered up almost instantly. As you have read throughout my story, the only times I had experienced "sober" since the beginning of high school was for brief periods when I was physically separated from drugs and alcohol. I didn't sleep that night. I tossed and turned. Every single incident in my life that I regretted flashed through my mind. I will never make it. I can't even stay sober in prison, how the hell am I going to make it back in the real world?

The following morning, I patiently waited for the yard to open so I could go to the library. I lived there during my free time. I read every book I could get my hands on. Reading took me out of the chaos within my mind. This day just felt different. I had a thought while walking to the library to go to the spirituality section. It happened to be the only section of the library that I had never entered. When I got there, the first book I saw had a man on the cover wrapped in an orangish-red sheet. This man had the biggest smile on his face that I had ever seen—literally from ear to ear. It was a book written by the Dhali Lama. I cannot remember the title of it, but I did read half of it that day. That night after taking my medication I sat up on my top bunk and wrapped a towel around my head and meditated for the first time. I followed the instructions in the book as best I could. During this period of meditation there were small windows of silence, of stillness. It was just enough to provide me with the hope to carry on the path of seeking. All the other inmates thought it was a joke. They nicknamed me "the Buddha," which surprisingly, I kind of enjoyed. It sure beat most other nicknames I had been handed throughout the years. Apparently, the rehab that I was accepted into had the reputation as the hardest treatment center in the country, maybe the world. It was a "Therapeutic Community." When I asked them to explain, they detailed, "You have to tell on each other all day, every day." Telling on people, at least from a convict's point of view, is the worst thing imaginable. There wasn't any lower action that you could engage in. I laughed it all off and tried to forget about it, until the day came. August 23, 2007. I remember it like it was yesterday.

-CHAPTER FOURTEEN-
LIBERATION OF SELF

Time will kill a man's mind
Especially in a cell so confined
No chance of freedom only through prayer
Looking to your corner to find no one is there

I waited impatiently in the processing center of the prison while the guard was checking me out. My adoptive mother and stepfather waited outside to receive me. I was so scared I couldn't sit still. I had this dark feeling that everything was going to fall apart again, I just didn't know how long it was going to take. I had no one other than my family as I had exploited everyone I had ever come into contact with. All these thoughts rushed through my mind. I wondered how many of the people I had burned were still looking for me? Was I going to be killed? Many of the individuals I had stolen from had threatened me before coming to prison. Was I going to get high again? Did rehab mean that I was never going to be able to numb the way that I felt inside again? All these thoughts passed the time as the guard processed my paperwork and went through my belongings. All of a sudden, I heard the guard say, "Crandall #39932, sign here to receive your property, sign here for the terms of your release." After my final signature, the guard popped open the first of three doors. He looked at me and said, "Good luck kid, I hope I never see you again, but probably will." Without response, I walked forward. I always had something sarcastic to say back to the guards. This day was different. Deep within I knew that his prediction was more than accurate. How long would it take?

Here it was, the moment I had been waiting two years to see. The sunshine, freedom, it wasn't how I had pictured it at all. I was absolutely terrified. I was so nervous my stomach was inside out. The final gate popped open and my adoptive mother greeted me with a big hug. I don't remember saying much as we drove nearly three hours to the treatment center that I was court-ordered to complete, or I would end up back in prison. I listened to music on my headset that I asked my mother to bring for the ride. I did not know what to say. Here were two individuals who had always been there for me no matter what actions I took against them or what hatred spewed from my lips. I'm sorry! Those words held no meaning coming from me. I had been sorry my whole life, but my actions never backed up my remorse. I was sorry, one sorry individual.

When we rolled into the treatment center, I was terrified. I knew that the fear was based on the fact that I had been abusing my medications for the entire two years of my prison sentence, and I had a full prescription in my back pack. I had been obsessing about not turning it over to staff upon arrival. I remember skipping med call that morning, as I wanted this day to actually be the day I got sober. There could have been some effects of not taking my medication enhancing what I was feeling. My stepfather parked the truck, and we all got out. My old survival instincts kicked in, and I began to act as if I wasn't scared. It was second nature to me. I had shown up to so many places similar to this in the past and found that the only way that I would make it through my sentence was to act as if I was untouchable. I had to act as if there was nothing wrong with me, and everyone else was fucked up. Not the greatest foundation to begin to build a new life, but you have to start with what you have, and what I had was years and years of walls built up to keep others from getting in. I knew that this way of being had not produced the results that I had always hoped it would, but I knew nothing else.

We walked inside and were met by staff. They all greeted and welcomed me in. I wasn't mentally present during most of the greeting processes as I was still obsessing about sneaking my pills into my room and seeing how many of them I could get up my nose. Staff pulled me into an office and began the intake process. It was time for me to say goodbye to my adoptive mother and stepfather. With my toughest of tough-guy persona, I said goodbye and went back to the intake process. My adoptive mother grabbed me by the arm and made a statement that crippled me in that moment. She looked me in the eyes and said, "Mark, you had better do this right because we are done helping you financially and emotionally. If this doesn't work for you, know that you cannot come home."

I was devastated. I had been plotting how I was going to get back home the entire ride to treatment. What was I going to do now? In that moment, it hit me. This statement was the foundation for a new life. I had no other options. My adoptive father was not going to take me in. Most people in my hometown wanted to hurt me. The curtain had been closed.

In that moment, everything flashed before me: my adoptive father making the statement that I was a disgrace to his name and my grandmother telling me if I made the news again she was going to disown me. I was hopeless inside. I knew I wasn't going to be able to stay sober, let alone not engage in future criminal activity. It was all I knew up until that point in my life. Regardless of how I was feeling, I had to put my masculine face back on. I couldn't show weakness, or the others in the treatment center would surely attempt to take advantage of me. I may have been clueless on how to stay sober, but institutions were one of my areas of specialty.

We finished the intake process and staff was about to show me to my room when a strange feeling came over me. I had a thought to give them my medications and explain to them that I couldn't take them any longer. These thoughts were not uncommon for me, or for any humans for that matter, but I rarely listened to them. In this moment, however, I did listen. I handed them my medications and explained to them that I wouldn't be taking them, that I had been abusing them for the past two years, and if I was actually going to attempt this thing called sobriety that I had to actually try to be sober.

The staff looked at me funny after telling them that I had been snorting my anti-depressants, but took them regardless. I had heard many people talk about this light that was at the end of the tunnel, but never quite understood the reference until this moment. There was a faint glimmer ahead of me. Unclear to me at the time, I was about to embark on a life-long quest of transformation. It surely felt strange to be honest, as I can remember this being only the second time I had done so, but it felt better than the way I had been living.

Treatment consisted of group after group, house meeting after house meeting, outside recovery meetings, meetings at the local church, and what they referred to as Learning Experiences. These Learning Experiences came about when my peers in the house would call me out on behaviors that were hindering my chances of staying sober and living a productive life. I was like a sitting duck with these things. I was being what they referred to as Confronted by my peers every moment of every day. I was a ticking time bomb. Peers were constantly up my ass, calling me out on swearing, being angry, my facial expressions, and an assortment of other institutionalized behaviors. I was constantly in trouble. I spent the majority of my time in treatment as an outcast from my peers. You could find me washing dishes for eight hours at a time, working in the yard, or scrubbing baseboards. They called it "On Status." It may sound miserable but the methodology of this treatment program was exactly what was needed to beat the shit out of all the belief systems that I had been using to survive up until this point. It took a few months in treatment for me to begin to see that these belief systems were not serving me; they really had caused nothing but struggles for me.

About six months into treatment I hated everyone. My day consisted of a steady stream of internal dialogue telling me to punch this person, runaway from treatment, get high, and the most fatal… You are worthless, just end it all. Every day I woke up miserable, hating life and all those around me. I just wanted it all to end. Each night I would lay my head on the pillow and fixate on past mistakes and how hopeless I was. I'm not sure if you've ever tried to go to sleep when all you could think about was how everyone who ever said they loved you had walked out of your life, but it's not easy to rest with those thoughts running through your mind. I had thought that treatment was going to be the answer for me, but I felt as if I was in worse shape sober than I was when I was on the run and wasted every moment of my consciousness.

At this point I was going to outside recovery meetings (which I couldn't stand), and Church two times per week but nothing was helping me. When I was at Church I would have moments of feeling comfortable in my skin, but as soon as I was back at the treatment facility I wanted to hang myself from a tree. I didn't understand what was wrong with me. Staff told me that if I didn't go back on medication they would be forced to send me back to prison. I pondered this proposition on several occasions. Surely it would be easier to be back in prison than talk about my fucking feelings and get told on for everything I did wrong. I really didn't want to take medications; I had my whole life, and they never worked. This was the end, the culmination for me. Suicidal thoughts were becoming more and more frequent. I knew enough to not share these thoughts with anyone, as I would end up in another facility. I was lost. At this point, most nights I was crying myself to sleep, wanting the pain to go away. I had always believed that suicide was for quitters, but now I could empathize with those who took their lives, if they had the screaming in their heads that I did.

There was a group of people that would come to the treatment center every Thursday night to facilitate an in-house recovery meeting. No one ever went to it. This was likely because people in the outside recovery community talked shit about them—saying they were crazy and took recovery a little too seriously. I remember this particular Thursday night vividly. I had been plotting my last stand. I was going to steal a van from the facility and drive it as fast as it would go into a tree. All day I had been consumed with these plans. I couldn't see another way out. I had tried everything, and nothing was working. Nothing was providing internal relief for me. There I stood in the kitchen after dinner that Thursday evening about six and a half months into my stay at the treatment facility, stealing cookies from the walk-in fridge and staring out the back door. There were people standing by their vehicles smoking cigarettes and drinking coffee and laughing. I watched them for weeks wondering what they were on. Surely, people couldn't be that happy *and* be sober. As the curiosity rose in me, a thought came to me—similar to the one that I had when I handed over all my pills during my intake into treatment. The feeling within was that I needed to attend this meeting before it was too late. "Too late" meaning that I was going to end up taking my own life.

One of those thoughts crept in that I usually ignored, "Go to the meeting Mark." For some reason, I listened. As I was walking to the meeting, I had another thought, to say a prayer. Up to that point I thought prayer was some mystical thing, a thing that I did not understand. Prayer had never worked for me, meaning I never got what I wanted when I asked for it. I said a prayer uncommon to anything I had said before, "God if you can hear me, please allow me to hear something in this meeting." I walked into that meeting and there were five to six men and one woman in the room. No one from the treatment center beside me was there. I sat down and a man walked over to me and introduced himself. The meeting opened with a prayer and a man spoke for around 40 minutes. What he shared about was nothing I had heard before. This man shared about how he had connected to a Power greater than himself and followed directions out of this recovery book and how his whole life was transformed. He spoke with so much confidence and conviction. This man talked about how he had contemplated taking his own life and how he did not see any other viable option to relieve the way he felt inside. Bob was his name. I felt a glimmer of hope. This man didn't talk about all the stuff that he lost and how life had become financially difficult for him. He talked about how he wanted to end his life and saw no end in sight. He made the statement that he went through some 12-Step process, and as a result, he slept like a baby—this was all I wanted to hear. I could not remember the last time I got a good night's sleep.

After the meeting was over, I walked up to Bob and told him that if he couldn't show me how to feel how he now does that I was going to end my life.

Bob agreed to help me and met me every week before the meeting at my treatment center and talked with me about transformation. He gave me very specific directions which I followed exactly as he asked. Something began to happen inside of me. I felt hopeful. The light at the end of the tunnel that people used to talk about became visible to me. Weeks rolled by, Bob and I went deeper and deeper into this transformation work held inside of the 12-Steps. Bob became my mentor, my spiritual advisor and one of my closest friends. He always had an answer for my questions. It was usually the opposite of what I was thinking, but I followed his direction closely and began to feel lighter. Bob guided me through the 12-Steps. I know, I know, many of you will have something to say about this. I did as well for many years. Get your God talk out of here. God has no business with a man like me. Besides, my grandmother told me for years I was going to Hell. In my mind Hell was a likely reality given the life I had been living.

Bob taught me about meditation and prayer, which would be my sword and shield as I navigated my way through this new life. I still didn't think that God wanted anything to do with me; Bob reassured me that I didn't need to believe in God, but needed to be willing to believe. I was willing; I had to be for my only other option was suicide. Drugs and alcohol had stopped providing me with the relief that they once did. As I went through the 12-Step process I shared with Bob things I had never shared with anyone. I talked with him about past situations, some of which are outlined in this book and some of which are not. I went all in. I had no choice, this was the last stop for me. Bob guided me to my first true surrender, a personal inventory (or the fourth step) and into the amends process.

I finished my first fourth step quickly as I was in trouble at my treatment center again and forced to sit at a table for eight hours per day. Things I hadn't thought of in years came up and I began to see things that I never had before. I began to see all the ways that I had been living and how ineffective they were. Bob showed me some truth about the way I had been living life and the magnitude of my selfishness.

One of the most profound truths for me, and still a distinction that I continue to draw light from is the extent to which I have played the victim surrounding my past. Through my years of education, transformation work, and introspection, I have discovered that there is a big difference between *being* a victim and *playing* a victim. I have been a victim of some circumstances that most children will never experience, nor should they, but I did. This makes me a victim of these circumstances.

Playing the victim, which I had been doing my entire life is based on me blaming current and past actions on these circumstances. Bob shared with me that if I wanted to be truly free on the inside I needed to shed the belief systems surrounding my childhood. This has become a life-long quest for me, and now a focus of much of my professional life to empower individuals to the same truth and freedom I have found — this is the main reason for writing this book. People have suggested for years that I would help millions of people by putting my story out into the world. Of course, then I didn't believe, but now I am fully in touch with how powerful the transformation was.

As I carried on with this new quest of self-actualization and empowerment I began to incorporate spiritual practices into my daily routine. I began to pray and meditate daily and use other tools to gauge my conduct day to day. Based upon the way I had been living life before this 12-Step process, it took constant effort for me to be honest and to treat people with love and respect. I was forced to humble myself and attempt to mend the ways in which I had treated people. This was a terrifying process for me as many of the amends that I needed to make could land me back in prison. I was on parole and if I were to land a new charge, I would undoubtedly go back. Regardless of the potential consequences I went out to the world on a quest to repair all the damage that I had caused others. Any consequences that may come as a result of these amends *had* to be better than the plan I had formulated before talking with Bob. I set up a couple of hundred conversations with people who I had come into contact with throughout my life. I sought forgiveness and asked how I might right my wrongs. Most of these did not go the way I had intended; many went much more smoothly than I could have ever envisioned.

I started painting and doing drywall work again — this was the only thing I knew up to this point. I quickly found out that I was much more skilled without heroin or alcohol. I was making good money, at least better than all my peers who were working alongside me in the treatment facility. Within a few weeks, I had saved enough money to get an apartment and started to focus on moving out on my own. The only decision that I hadn't made was whether or not I wanted to move back home to be around my family. I discussed this with Bob, and he recommended that I stay local and carry on with the spiritual path that I had recently been introduced to. A man that I became close to within the community was moving out of his apartment and asked me if I was interested in renting it. Obviously, I was; I just wanted to get out of treatment. Nothing could be worse than some of the places that I had slept before.

—CHAPTER FIFTEEN—

MY NEW FRIEND

As I envision what my mind can't shake
Up to this point my life's been a big mistake
Left with distorted feelings in my head
Every morning I wake I dread

I ended up putting a down payment on the apartment the day I went to go look at it. Monday morning, I told my counselor Balinda that I was moving out in two weeks. She was upset and scared for me, but my fear had gone away. I was starting to feel happy on a daily basis. Most of my time was spent in the company other individuals who were attempting to live in the realm of the Spirit. I needed these individuals, as I still had thoughts of robbing and assaulting people. My new friend, God, (easier than saying Higher Power or Spirit of the Universe) had other plans for me.

I drove all over the state to talk to others suffering from the same things I had found release from. I was on a mission for increased self-liberation. I found that the more I engaged in these practices—workshops, webinars, and thousands of conversations—the more I recognized that the effect produced was similar to that of drugs or alcohol. All these things made me feel good inside, really good. The only difference was that the effects of these practices grew stronger and stronger, unlike the effects of drugs and alcohol, which decrease the more, you use them.

I moved out on my own, and many people who had come into my life donated furniture and other things that I would need. My apartment was on a river. I would sit out on the back porch each morning and listen to the calming sounds of the fast-moving water. Things were going well for me. I was working overtime and saving money. Unfortunately, I didn't anticipate that when it got cold, work dried up and most painting and dry wall companies would lay off their employees until the spring. At the time, I was blind to how dark times were about to get for me. Work began to slow down as the cold came in. The anniversary of some of the most traumatic moments of my life were approaching. I started to panic; flashes of homelessness and the necessity to resort back to my old life style plagued my daily thoughts. I would get quiet and these thoughts would drift, and then they would come back even stronger.

Eventually we were all laid off from work, and I found myself with a couple of thousand dollars saved and no work or plan on the horizon. Halloween approached and I started to think about my biological mother and her birthday. It was also the anniversary of my adoption. I started spending each day doing nothing but thinking about my past. Things got very dark, very quickly, for me. I started reliving all the most traumatic moments of my life.

Here I was, wrapped in fear about my upcoming homelessness, thinking about all the abuse and neglect of my childhood and isolated from those I had been spending a majority of my time with. Of course, all this was on top of my newfound awareness of all the harm that I had caused other people throughout my life. I began to experience an extreme depression. I stopped calling people and spent most of my days watching videos on the Internet and writing and reading poetry. Bob suggested that I increase my spiritual practices, which I did. I began to ask the Universe what my next move was to be. I did this day after day. Every time I caught myself in these dark thinking patterns, I would ask what my next move was supposed to be. It is not my intention to lead you to believe that I was in a constant state of positive thinking. This was one of the bleakest times for me. Some days it was a real struggle for me to get out of bed and do anything at all.

Bob called me one evening and asked me if I would fill in for him on a commitment with this man named Jim. Bob made the joke that I should be careful though, he was gay and might try to fuck me. This was a shock to me as I knew Jim and did not know he was gay. He didn't paint his nails or flip his hair in the wind. He dressed strange but I just figured it was because he was an artist. Regardless of his sexuality I needed to go help someone. I was losing my mind. Jim picked me up that evening and we headed to the meeting where we were going to share our experience. The conversation was light on the way there. I remember thinking that homosexuality was contagious. Like he was going to sneeze on me, and I would start wearing leather pants and a pink shirt.

On the way back to my apartment, Jim and I started talking. I had an overwhelming feeling that I should let him know that there would be zero chance of us becoming friends. In that moment, I turned to Jim and said, "I just want you to know that I hate faggots." Jim looked back at me and said, "Interesting, let's talk about that." I shared with him the time I learned of a family member's attraction to men when I snooped on his computer. I read through a gay chat site where he discussed sexual acts with another man. This was a secret I had been holding onto, because if it were known, it could devastate my family. As Jim and I discussed this, I realized that we were parked in my driveway. We had been talking for a while. Jim and I shifted the conversation to discussing art. I told him of all the poetry I had written and how much I loved art. We made plans to meet up and get lunch and share art with each other.

Jim would become one of my closest friends. To this day, I have a connection with him greater than I have experienced with another man. It is through our friendship that I am able to share this story with you. He told me "you are an artist and your job is to put your art out into the world. The world gets to determine what it means to them."

—CHAPTER SIXTEEN—

STUDENT LOANS

Self-esteem is like a maple tree
Waiting to be tapped
Nourish it
For it is the sweetest of sap

A couple of months into the practice of asking the Universe what direction I was to head, I began to start thinking about College. I started to look into schools and areas of study that interested me. I wanted to go to school online due to my lack of self-esteem, specifically about my intelligence. My experience with education was that I didn't do very well at it. Of course, this was mainly due to the influence of drugs and alcohol. I felt as if I should go to school for business. Maybe I could start my own painting and drywall company. This would ensure that I was not laid-off during winters. I booked a couple of phone interviews with schools and after several conversations I narrowed down my choice. While on the phone with the enrollment counselor, she asked me what I wanted to study. I told her that I wanted to study psychology. This baffled me as I had already made up my mind that I was going to study business. Although I had an overwhelming feeling that I may have made the wrong decision, I went with it.

Turns out, when you take away the drugs and alcohol, I was a pretty intelligent person. My GPA stayed around 4.0. The assignments were easy. I spent that entire winter doing odd jobs and working on psychology homework. Jim approached me about doing some drywall work for him. This job would take me a few days and provide me with the money to pay my rent. I was extremely fearful that I was not going to be able to pay my rent so I started the same day he showed me what he needed to have done.

When I completed the work a few days later, I had a thought to steal some money from Jim. The strange thing was that I had money, and he was paying me handsomely for the work I had done. It was not as if I would not be able to eat dinner that night. But, I took two pockets full of quarters from him. I cannot explain why I did this other than it was another attempt to feed the hole within me. And … it did all but that. It was all I could think about. This decision haunted me. I held onto it for a couple of weeks before I finally called Bob and told him what I had done. He directed me to set up a meeting with Jim and pay him back the money. Bob also questioned me about the amends I was unwilling to make at that time. Could this lack of action be preventing me from overcoming my need to steal from others? This hit me hard, as I did not want to make these amends. I had six burglary and two robbery amends left to make. I was not convicted for these, but if convicted, I would be a career criminal and face a minimum of 7 1/2 to 15 years in prison.

Although I had applied the practices of "telling on myself," and "asking forgiveness for my sins," I still felt horrible about what I had done. I've always been extremely judgmental of myself, but it seemed to intensify when sober. Maybe it had always been as intense, I just didn't realize it as much due to the fact that I was minimizing my consciousness through substance abuse. I hated myself for the fact that I had hurt another person who I cared about. What was wrong with me? Would I ever be normal?

I reached out to Jim and asked if he would be willing to get dinner with me that night. He agreed, and we met up. I was terrified because I had never owned up to stealing after engaging in the act before now. I pulled $40 out of my pocket and handed it to him, and explained what I had done and asked if there was anything else I could do to make this right. He was very receptive, said that he forgave me, and didn't view me any differently. He may not have, but I sure did. I was a thief—always had been and likely would never change. You know the old saying, "once a thief, always a thief."

Eulogy Of Childhood Memories

CHAPTER SEVENTEEN

REDEMPTION

Freedoms at my fingertips once and for all
Never again for this addiction will I crawl
As another day passes me by
"Just for today" I see no reason to die

A couple of weeks after my attempt at rectifying yet another mistake, I decided to set up a meeting with my parole officer. I had been guided to tell him about stealing from Jim and how I needed to make amends back home and to seek his guidance on how to navigate this without ending up back in prison. I set up an appointment for the following morning. I spent that entire day and night worrying about if he would send me back to prison. I stole and was about to confess to a bunch of crimes, why would he not send me back? When I walked in he told me to sit down, and so I did. He said, "What's this all about?" I told him everything. I poured it out as quick as I could because I figured my willingness to be honest had a shelf life. He kicked his feet up on his desk and said "Mark, if you are arrested for any of these, I will make sure you don't see another day in prison. You, my friend, are ready to get off parole. I will submit the paperwork for early termination." I headed home that weekend and made 10 amends. I was on fire. My depressive thoughts were gone. I had purpose. I was on a mission to help people and discover more and more internal freedom.

A few weeks later my paperwork came in the mail indicating that I had been released from parole three and a half years early due to good behavior. I could not believe it! Why had I not experienced this amazing life the several other times I wanted to stop getting high and drunk? It didn't matter—now was my time, and I needed to continue to seek God's will, for this new life was a direct result of seeking more and more of this spiritual life. Thoughts of moving to a bigger area with more opportunity came into my meditation practice for a few weeks straight, so I decided to take some action and see if there was any validity to it. I followed through and started reaching out to friends to see if they had rooms for rent. After some time, I moved to the Seacoast and around the same time enrolled into an actual University to finish out my undergraduate degree. After moving, I quickly and easily obtained a position on a painting crew, making good money. I began to save all my earnings outside of what I needed to live. I was tired of living paycheck to paycheck. It became an obsession to see how much money I could save. My Oma used to tell me that I needed to have six months of all my expenses put away because you never knew what life was going to hand you. In the back of my mind, every dollar I didn't have saved meant I was that much closer to being homeless again.

It didn't take me long to become engulfed in the recovery community on the Seacoast. I made many friends, some of which I still have today. One of these friends wanted me to attend a young people's recovery conference in New York with her and some other people. I wasn't excited about this invite due to how socially awkward I could still be sometimes. I didn't want to go and told her this. She insisted that I go, and I gave in. It was absolute chaos at this conference. People were screaming and banging on drums. Total shenanigans! After making our way through the hotel to our room, I calmed down. In the hotel room, a good friend of mine and I decided to meditate to ground ourselves. As we were meditating the door opened. There were three women that informed us that they were going to be staying in the hotel room with us. One of these women was the most beautiful thing I had ever set my eyes upon. We stared at each other for a moment, and then they walked out of the room, and my friend and I continued to meditate. As the conference rolled on I began to have fun. I was hanging out and talking with people and "letting my hair down."

The first night of the conference I ended up sleeping in

the same bed as the woman I had a moment with in the hotel room earlier that day. This may sound romantic, but there were like 12 people staying in that hotel room. Three or four of which were in each bed in the room. That woman's name was Megan. Megan and I laid next to each other and talked that evening and even cuddled a bit. We didn't talk after that until the following evening. I searched for her all day. There was a pit in my stomach that I hadn't felt since Karen dumped me back in high school. I hated this feeling. It reminded me of all those times my biological mother would claim that she was coming to visit and then never show up.

I came to find out that Megan had driven from New York back to Pennsylvania for a funeral. She returned late that evening. I was sitting in the main room in which the big recovery meeting was to be held. She walked in with her other two friends. She was gorgeous. My heart melted, and I became giddy with joy. She sat next to me and we talked. After the meeting, we decided to walk around the city. We talked and walked for hours and hours. I stole a few kisses, and we held hands as we walked. The moment which changed me forever was when a homeless man asked us for money. I sat down next to him on the dirty sidewalk and talked with him. Megan sat down next to me without hesitation. I fell in love. We stayed up all night together. We exchanged phone numbers and have not stopped being together and growing spiritually since that night.

A few months later, I moved in with Megan and we started to build our lives together. We hardly ever fought and when we did have disagreements they were short lived and usually ended with us laughing at each other. Shortly after moving in with Megan I started my final classes of my undergraduate degree. I started to seek positions in the field of Human Services in which I had been studying. It was a terrifying process due to the extensive criminal background that I had accrued as a result of my drug addiction and alcoholism. I was facing extreme difficulty even finding an agency that would allow me to come in and interview. I had no practical experience working in the field of Human Services. The only thing that I had working for me was my knowledge and experiences of "living in the dark side." I later found, and it is continually revealed to me how beneficial all of my darkest experiences are in the light of empowering others to change.

The first couple of weeks in my final classes, it was suggested that I find a mentor, someone to help guide me in the field. One of my professors had intrigued me. Here was a man with an overwhelming personality, so much confidence, and intelligence. I walked up him on one of the breaks and asked him to guide me, to help me make my way. His name was Marvin. He asked me several questions and then told me to meet him for lunch, and so I did. This man called a friend of his and asked if she would interview me for a position working with runaway and homeless youth. She agreed to interview me and I nailed it. During the interview, I tapped into skills I was oblivious to at the time and started interviewing the youth that was there to interview me. I was hired for the position and although I didn't know it then, my entire life was about to change forever.

The job that I was hired for allowed me to work with runaway and homeless youth at a drop-in center. The first year of this job was fun, difficult, and brought up all my childhood traumas. I would often go home so distraught that I didn't know if I would be able to go to work the following day. I continued to practice meditation and other introspection/transformational work which allowed me to overcome these blocks and go further and further as a professional and a spiritual being. I had spent much of my life not being able to fall asleep at night. Due to the Realm of the Spirit that Bob introduced me to, I sleep soundly at night. I currently have no one that I knowingly owe amends to. I don't owe anyone money—I have made hundreds of amends to people and businesses in which I had stolen from.

Marvin stayed a mentor of mine for years. He became a huge influence on my professional and spiritual life. After two and a half years I decided to seek new employment. I wanted to work at the youth detention center, but knew they would never hire a felon. I applied anyway, the power of God had smashed my beliefs before by creating possibility in the wake of self-judgment, so why not now. I applied and was hired, one of very few felons hired by the State. The grass was not greener on the other side of the fence, however. I hated working there. Having lived in similar institutions as a youth, I was unable to separate myself enough from my empathy for the youth I was working with. My difficulties were intensified by the fact that the gossip spread surrounding my criminal past. Some of my co-workers were supportive of me, while others avoided me. Someone even went so far as to notify the local newspaper and tell them that I was hired. They wrote an article about how the State had hired a convict to oversee youth. Some of my coworkers felt as if this should have bothered me more than it did. I viewed this as God showing others what he had led me to walk through as a pure demonstration of His power. To me this was a huge demonstration of the power of spiritual practices.

-CHAPTER EIGHTEEN-

MARRIAGE

I thought it was the end
Then I felt you by my side
With you in my corner
Never again will I hide

Megan and I had been together for about one and a half years at this point, and I knew it was nearing time to ask her to marry me. I was pretty resistant to marriage until this point, as I had seen very few, if any, last for life as most all wedding vows state. I sought the counsel of one of the pastors of a church where one of my recovery meetings was hosted. At this time, I also had a new spiritual advisor. His name is Brian. Brian had been married for years and has a couple of children. He navigated his relationship with so much love and grace, I prayed that I could someday have something that beautiful. I had countless conversations regarding marrying Megan. I decided it was time. I was never in a million years going to find another woman as strong, passionate, and beautiful as the one I had. I asked both of her fathers for their permission to marry her. They gave me their blessings, and her mother even sent me a set of rings she had if I wanted to use them. I was so terrified that as soon as the rings arrived in the mail I opened the package and proposed. I was supposed to wait and do it in Aruba on a family trip, but I could not. We were married on September 8, 2012, one of the greatest days of my life.

I graduated from the University of New Hampshire with a Master's Degree in Social Work (MSW). I was planning to take the easier route of obtaining my degree through an easier program but Marvin insisted that I was smart enough to obtain my MSW. This three-year program was one of the most difficult tasks I had undertaken in since entering recovery. Both of my adoptive parents were in attendance. The relationships that I have with them today are amazing. I know that if my life had taken a different turn, I would not be the strong man that I am now.

Megan and I ended up moving to Austin, Texas, several years later in attempt to avoid winter. Well, we thought it was to avoid winter; God always has a plan even if I'm unaware of his workings at the time. Since arriving we have witnessed nothing but the most amazing opportunities. My life is more beautiful than I could have ever imagined. On August 23, 2007, the day I walked out of New Hampshire State Prison, the fear that I experienced that day would be the fuel in which I would rebuild my life. I have done and continue to do work each and every day to break away from the life I once lived.

The greatest distinction that I have found throughout all the introspection work that I have done is the difference between *being* a victim and *playing* one. I have stopped playing the victim. In the future, I plan to publish another piece on the path I follow to solidify this distinction in my daily life.

As a result of moving to Austin, I have been placed in the paths of some brilliantly motivating individuals. I have embarked on a quest that God put in my heart at 18 years old to become an author, motivational speaker, and mindset coach. I've started a business coaching individuals to overcome their limiting beliefs and begin to live truly powerful lives. The more coaching, speaking and entrepreneurial endeavors I indulge in, the more I tap into my true power. My business has flourished and as a result has laid the groundwork for me to help countless individuals.

Who would have thought that all my mistakes and misfortunes would one day develop into the foundation of helping others live more fulfilling lives. As a result of my guidance, to devote my life to helping others, I have started several businesses focused on coaching individuals to overcome any and all limiting beliefs preventing them from living the life of their dreams. This has turned into some amazing conversations surrounding the possibility of transforming self-hatred to love, increasing the success of their businesses, discovering and following their true callings. My experience has been that most people spend their lives trapped in would've, could've, should've. I've devoted my life's work to ending regret and accomplishing everything there is to accomplish in this life. I hope that my story inspires you to tap into your true potential and not allow situations from your past, any limiting belief, any self-judgment stop you from fully living up to that potential.

The guiding force in devoting my time to writing this book was the possibility of it touching the lives of millions of individuals that believe that their past will dictate their future. This has not been the case for me thus far in life and I sincerely hope it is not so for you. I am grateful for all the darkest points of my life, each of these have allowed me the opportunity for spiritual growth. I will end this story with a quote:

"Failure is a word reserved by those that have quit."
- Mark Crandall

Although this story has come to an end, I really view this as a beginning. Over the past 10+ years I have tapped into the power that is stored within spiritual practices and transformation work, and I want more and more of it. I have created the possibility through my trials and tribulations— touching the lives of millions of people and empowering them to take the actions necessary to transform their own lives. If there is one thing that has become extremely clear to me it is that we are not promised tomorrow. This exact moment is all we have. Yet I spent most of my life on layaway—always putting things off as if I'm promised the opportunity to complete them at a later time , but we only get one of these things called life.

ACKNOWLEDGMENTS

The process of writing these accounts was one of the most difficult of my existence. To all of those who have been by my side since the beginning and those that stayed with me through the darkest times of my life, thank you—I owe you my life. Although many "friendships" did not make it through the trials and tribulations of my first 22 years of life, my family did!

Tim, thank you for being patient with me and teaching me the importance of art. Without your friendship I would never of had the courage to write and release my story to the world for their interpretation. It took some years to realize it, but I am truly blessed to have 2 sets of family. Both of which supported me the best they could.

My wife Megan, the strongest woman that I know and the greatest life companion a man could ask for. Megan, you have loved me through this process from the ups to the downs and back again.

My Spiritual Advisor, Brian, you have talked me through some of the biggest fears I have ever experienced. You've taught me how to be a man and demonstrated what it means to be a loving husband and father.

Marty, I thank you for believing in me, loving me and pushing me when I couldn't see the greatness within. Without you this book would surely not have been written nor would I be the man I am today.

Additional thanks to the men who have pushed me when I wanted to quit and who continued to take action in their own lives, helping to propel me forward; my mom and dad, for taking me into your home and adopting me as your own and for being two of the most amazing souls I have encountered on this earth; my sister, Shannon, who has always been there for me and supported me no matter how I showed up to the relationship.

ABOUT THE AUTHOR

A native of New Hampshire, Mark Crandall now lives in Austin, Texas, where he is a Mindset Coach, Author, and Motivational Speaker.

His first book, *Eulogy of Childhood Memories*, is Crandall's memoir of mastering an unstoppable mind state and empowering as many individuals as possible to achieve the same mental freedom and accomplishment he has found.

Mark was taken from his biological parents at the age of 3 and placed into foster care. He spent the next 20 years of his life trying to find himself while navigating through drug addiction, behavioral outbursts, and numerous institutions.

In 2007 Crandall made the decision to transform his life. He refused to be plagued by his past.

Since that time, he has spent thousands on meditation retreats and transformational workshops, studying self-help books as well as seeking the best therapy in the nation.

Crandall obtained his Bachelors Degree in Human Services and his Masters Degree in Social Work from The University of New Hampshire.

He has found through all of his studies that your thoughts are the only things that can defeat you. Outside of your thoughts nothing holds meaning. The only meaning that life holds is created with in your mind.

One of the greatest distinctions that Crandall works with, himself, and with his clients is that there is a difference between "being a victim" and "playing a victim." Mark was a victim in the sense that he had things happen to him throughout his life that he cannot change. Today, he no longer "plays the victim," meaning he no longer attributes his current reactions/actions in life to his past trauma or misfortunes.

"Failure is a word reserved by those that have quit."
-Mark Crandall

Made in the USA
Middletown, DE
20 March 2019